The Ithaca Manual of Style

Writing Fiction and Nonfiction
that is Clear, Concise, and Captivating

by

Michael Pastore

Zorba Press
Ithaca, New York, USA
www.ZorbaPress.com

ISBN+13: 9780927379069

Library of Congress Control Number: 2014903635

Published by Zorba Press, February 2016.
Printed and bound in the United States of America.
Cover photo (of Ithaca Falls) by Michael Pastore.

About the Book, *The Ithaca Manual of Style:*
Most traditional style guides are mere reference books containing countless tedious rules and reminders about SPUG: spelling, punctuation, usage, and grammar. *The Ithaca Manual of Style* is not about the fanatic obsession with correctness. In a lively style, *The Ithaca Manual* illuminates how professional writers write with precision, power, energy, and passion.

This book's companion website — Publishers Cafe —
contains resources for writers, readers, editors, and publishers:
www.publisherscafe.com

For sales, permissions, and all other inquiries,
please contact Zorba Press by email at
books@zorbapress.com

Or, visit Zorba Press on the Web:
                    www.ZorbaPress.com

Printings: cv003/ip014

Contents

A. Reading Makes Us Human

B. The Writer's Art, Craft, and Personal Struggle

C. One Word Is Better Than Two

D. The Style is the Woman Herself

Resources and Sources

Resources

For resources about writing, editing, publishing, reading, and literary style, visit this book's companion website:

Publishers Cafe
http://www.publisherscafe.com

Sources of the Essays

An asterisk (*) indicates that the essay reprinted here is not complete: the most interesting and significant selections have been chosen by the editor.

4] Ruskin's essay* is from his book *Sesame and Lilies.*

6] Many of the quotes are from the anthology, *Zenlightenment.*

8] The Anatole France selection is from *The Opinions of Anatole France,* recorded by Paul Gsell.

9] Arnold Bennett's essay is from is his book *The Author's Craft.*

13] The Balzac selection is from his novel, *Cousin Bette.*

20] The essay *On Jargon,* * by Quiller-Couch, first delivered as a lecture, is now included in his book, *On the Art of Writing.*

21] Twain's rules are selected from his essay, *Fenimore Cooper's Literary Offenses.* *

25] Thoreau's perfectly healthy sentences are from his book *A Week on the Concord and Merrimack Rivers.*

26] The pieces by Whitman are from his *Preface to the 1855 Edition of Leaves of Grass;* and *A Backward Glance O'er Travel'd Roads (1888).*

27] Shaw's instructive outburst is from the Preface to his drama *Man and Superman.*

29] *On Familiar Style,* * by William Hazlitt.

Clearness, simplicity, conciseness.

— Leo Tolstoy

The written word is clean as bone,
Clear as light, Firm as stone
Two words are not
As good as one.

— Anonymous

Often turn the stile (make corrections carefully),
if you expect to write anything worthy
of being read twice.

— Horace

People think that I can teach them style. What stuff it is! Have something
to say and say it as clearly as you can. That is the only secret of style.

— Matthew Arnold

It makes a great difference to the force of any sentence, whether there be
a man behind it, or no. In the learned journal, in the influential newspaper,
I discern no form; only some irresponsible shadow; oftener some monied
corporation, or some dangler, who hopes, in the mask and robes of his
paragraph, to pass for somebody. But, through every clause and part of
speech of a right book, I meet the eyes of the most determined of men: his
force and terror inundate every word: the commas and dashes are alive; so
that the writing is athletic and nimble, — can go far and live long.

— Ralph Waldo Emerson

Don't tell me the moon is shining;
show me the glint of light on broken glass.

— Anton Chekhov

What is style? ... It is more, vastly more, than the sum of the diction (the choice and use of words), the syntax (the arrangement of words in phrases and sentences), and the careful crafting of sentences to transmit an idea or evoke a feeling. Style, in great writing, is the sincerest expression of the author's inmost self. Great style is clear, concise, and captivating — nothing is lacking, nothing is superfluous. Whenever we read great writing something genuine in it moves us, in waves of resonance and recognition, with rays of wonder and delight.

— Michael Pastore

Carlyle noted of Goethe, "his emblematic intellect, his never-failing tendency to transform into *shape,* into *life,* the feeling that may dwell in him. Everything has form, has visual excellence: the poet's imagination bodies forth the forms of things unseen, and his pen turns them into shape."

— Sir Arthur Quiller-Couch

The way to write well is to live intensely.

— Virginia Woolf

Who can doubt that Plato wins us to his wisdom by that skin and body of poetry in which Sir Philip declares his philosophy is clothed? ... The scene opens in Old Athens, which his genius continues for us ever new; the morning dawns; a breeze from the Aegean flutters upon our foreheads; the rising sun tips the friezes of the Parthenon, and gradually slants upon the house in whose yet whose twilight courts gather a company of white-vested, whispering guests "expecting till that fountain of wisdom, " Protagoras, should arise.

— Edward Fitzgerald

How can we manage it that all be fresh, and new and pleasing and instructive, at once?

— Goethe

1
Reading

by Henry David Thoreau

From: *Life Without Principle*

Not without a slight shudder at the danger, I often perceive how near I had come to admitting into my mind the details of some trivial affair, — the news of the street; and I am astonished to observe how willing men are to lumber their minds with such rubbish, — to permit idle rumors and incidents of the most insignificant kind to intrude on ground which should be sacred to thought. Shall the mind be a public arena, where the affairs of the street and the gossip of the tea-table chiefly are discussed? Or shall it be a quarter of heaven itself, — an hypaethral temple, consecrated to the service of the gods?

From: *A Week on the Concord and Merrimack Rivers*

Read the best books first, or you may not have a chance to read them at all. ... Certainly, we do not need to be soothed and entertained always like children. He who resorts to the easy novel, because he is languid, does no better than if he took a nap. ... Books, not which afford us a cowering enjoyment, but in which each thought is of unusual daring; such as an idle man cannot read, and a timid one would not be entertained by, which even make us dangerous to existing institutions,—such call I good books.

There is a chasm between knowledge and ignorance which the arches of science can never span. A book should contain pure discoveries, glimpses of *terra firma,* though by shipwrecked mariners, and not the art of navigation by those who have never been out of sight of land. *They* must not yield wheat and potatoes, but must themselves be the unconstrained and natural harvest of their author's lives.

We do not learn much from learned books, but from true, sincere, human books ...

From: *Walden — or, Life in the Woods*

With a little more deliberation in the choice of their pursuits, all men would perhaps become essentially students and observers, for certainly their nature and destiny are interesting to all alike. In accumulating property for ourselves or our posterity, in founding a family or a state, or acquiring fame even, we are mortal; but in dealing with truth we are immortal, and need fear no change nor accident. The oldest Egyptian or Hindoo philosopher raised a corner of the veil from the statue of the divinity; and still the trembling robe remains raised, and I gaze upon as fresh a glory as he did, since it was I in him that was then so bold, and it is he in me that now reviews the vision. No dust has settled on that robe; no time has elapsed since that divinity was revealed. That time which we really improve, or which is improvable, is neither past, present, nor future.

My residence was more favorable, not only to thought, but to serious reading, than a university; and though I was beyond the range of the ordinary circulating library, I had more than ever come within the influence of those books which circulate round the world, whose sentences were first written on bark, and are now merely copied from time to time on to linen paper. Says the poet Mîr Camar Uddîn Mast, "Being seated to run through the region of the spiritual world; I have had this advantage in books. To be intoxicated by a single glass of wine; I have experienced this pleasure when I have drunk the liquor of the esoteric doctrines." I kept Homer's Iliad on my table through the summer, though I looked at his page only now and then. Incessant labor with my hands, at first, for I had my house to finish and my beans to hoe at the same time, made more study impossible. Yet I sustained myself by the prospect of such reading in future. I read one or two shallow books of travel in the intervals of my work, till that employment made me ashamed of myself, and I asked where it was then that *I* lived.

The student may read Homer or Aeschylus in the Greek without danger of dissipation or luxuriousness, for it implies that he in some measure emulate their heroes, and consecrate morning hours to their pages. The heroic books, even if printed in the character of our mother tongue, will always be in a language dead to degenerate times; and we must laboriously seek the meaning of each word and line, conjecturing a larger sense than common use permits out of what wisdom and valor and generosity we have. The modern cheap and fertile press, with all its translations, has done little to bring us nearer to the heroic writers of antiquity. They seem as solitary, and the letter in which they are printed as rare and curious, as ever. It is worth the expense of youthful days and costly hours, if you learn only some words of an ancient language, which are raised out of the trivialness of the street, to be perpetual suggestions and provocations. It is not in vain that the farmer remembers and repeats the few Latin words which he has heard. Men sometimes speak as if the study of the classics would at length make way for more modern and practical studies; but the adventurous student will always study classics, in whatever language they may be written and however ancient they may be. For what are the classics but the noblest recorded thoughts of man? They are the only oracles which are not decayed, and there are such answers to the most modern inquiry in them as Delphi and Dodona never gave. We might as well omit to study Nature because she is old. To read well, that is, to read true books in a true spirit, is a noble exercise, and one that will task the reader more than any exercise which the customs of the day esteem. It requires a training such as the athletes underwent, the steady intention almost of the whole life to this object. Books must be read as deliberately and reservedly as they were written. It is not enough even to be able to speak the language of that nation by which they are written, for there is a memorable interval between the spoken and the written language, the language heard and the language read. The one is commonly transitory, a sound, a tongue, a dialect merely, almost brutish, and we learn it unconsciously, like the brutes, of our mothers. The other is the maturity and experience of that; if that is our mother tongue, this is our father tongue, a reserved and select expression, too significant to be heard by the ear, which we must be born again in order to speak. The crowds of men who merely *spoke* the Greek and Latin tongues in the middle ages were not entitled by the accident of birth to *read* the works of genius written in those languages; for these were not written in that Greek or Latin which they knew, but in the select language of literature. They had not learned the nobler dialects of Greece and Rome, but the very materials on which they were written were waste paper to them, and they prized instead a cheap contemporary literature. But when the several nations of Europe had acquired distinct though rude written languages of their own, sufficient for the purposes of their rising literatures, then first learning revived, and scholars were enabled to discern from that remoteness the treasures of antiquity. What the Roman and Grecian multitude could not *hear,* after the lapse of ages a few scholars *read,* and a few scholars only are still reading it.

However much we may admire the orator's occasional bursts of eloquence, the noblest written words are commonly as far behind or above the fleeting spoken language as the firmament with its stars is behind the clouds. *There* are the stars, and they who can may read them. The astronomers forever comment on and observe them. They are not exhalations like our daily colloquies and vaporous breath. What is called eloquence in the forum is commonly found to be rhetoric in the study. The orator yields to the inspiration of a transient occasion, and speaks to the mob before him, to those who can *hear* him; but the writer, whose more equable life is his occasion, and who would be distracted by the event and the crowd which inspire the orator, speaks to the intellect and heart of mankind, to all in any age who can *understand* him.

No wonder that Alexander carried the Iliad with him on his expeditions in a precious casket. A written word is the choicest of relics. It is something at once more intimate with us and more universal than any other work of art. It is the work of art nearest to life itself. It may be translated into every language, and not only be read but actually breathed from all human lips; — not be represented on canvas or in marble only, but be carved out of the breath of life itself. The symbol of an ancient man's thought becomes a modern man's speech. Two thousand summers have imparted to the monuments of Grecian literature, as to her marbles, only a maturer golden and autumnal tint, for they have carried their own serene and celestial atmosphere into all lands to protect them against the corrosion of time. Books are the treasured wealth of the world and the fit inheritance of generations and nations. Books, the oldest and the best, stand naturally and rightfully on the shelves of every cottage. They have no cause of their own to plead, but while they enlighten and sustain the reader his common sense will not refuse them. Their authors are a natural and irresistible aristocracy in every society, and, more than kings or emperors, exert an influence on mankind. When the illiterate and perhaps scornful trader has earned by enterprise and industry his coveted leisure and independence, and is admitted to the circles of wealth and fashion, he turns inevitably at last to those still higher but yet inaccessible circles of intellect and genius, and is sensible only of the imperfection of his culture and the vanity and insufficiency of all his riches, and further proves his good sense by the pains which he takes to secure for his children that intellectual culture whose want he so keenly feels; and thus it is that he becomes the founder of a family.

Those who have not learned to read the ancient classics in the language in which they were written must have a very imperfect knowledge of the history of the human race; for it is remarkable that no transcript of them has ever been made into any modern tongue, unless our civilization itself may be regarded as such a transcript. Homer has never yet been printed in English, nor Aeschylus, nor Virgil even, — works as refined, as solidly done, and as beautiful almost as the morning itself; for later writers, say what we will of their genius, have rarely, if ever, equalled the elaborate beauty and finish and the lifelong and heroic literary labors of the ancients.

They only talk of forgetting them who never knew them. It will be soon enough to forget them when we have the learning and the genius which will enable us to attend to and appreciate them. That age will be rich indeed when those relics which we call Classics, and the still older and more than classic but even less known Scriptures of the nations, shall have still further accumulated, when the Vaticans shall be filled with Vedas and Zendavestas and Bibles, with Homers and Dantes and Shakspeares, and all the centuries to come shall have successively deposited their trophies in the forum of the world. By such a pile we may hope to scale heaven at last.

The works of the great poets have never yet been read by mankind, for only great poets can read them. They have only been read as the multitude read the stars, at most astrologically, not astronomically. Most men have learned to read to serve a paltry convenience, as they have learned to cipher in order to keep accounts and not be cheated in trade; but of reading as a noble intellectual exercise they know little or nothing; yet this only is reading, in a high sense, not that which lulls us as a luxury and suffers the nobler faculties to sleep the while, but what we have to stand on tiptoe to read and devote our most alert and wakeful hours to.

I think that having learned our letters we should read the best that is in literature, and not be forever repeating our a b abs, and words of one syllable, in the fourth or fifth classes, sitting on the lowest and foremost form all our lives. Most men are satisfied if they read or hear read, and perchance have been convicted by the wisdom of one good book, the Bible, and for the rest of their lives vegetate and dissipate their faculties in what is called easy reading. There is a work in several volumes in our Circulating Library entitled Little Reading, which I thought referred to a town of that name which I had not been to. There are those who, like cormorants and ostriches, can digest all sorts of this, even after the fullest dinner of meats and vegetables, for they suffer nothing to be wasted. If others are the machines to provide this provender, they are the machines to read it. They read the nine thousandth tale about Zebulon and Sephronia, and how they loved as none had ever loved before, and neither did the course of their true love run smooth, — at any rate, how it did run and stumble, and get up again and go on! how some poor unfortunate got up onto a steeple, who had better never have gone up as far as the belfry; and then, having needlessly got him up there, the happy novelist rings the bell for all the world to come together and hear, O dear! how he did get down again! For my part, I think that they had better metamorphose all such aspiring heroes of universal noveldom into man weathercocks, as they used to put heroes among the constellations, and let them swing round there till they are rusty, and not come down at all to bother honest men with their pranks. The next time the novelist rings the bell I will not stir though the meeting-house burn down. "The Skip of the Tip-Toe-Hop, a Romance of the Middle Ages, by the celebrated author of 'Tittle-Tol-Tan,' to appear in monthly parts; a great rush; don't all come together." All this they read with saucer eyes, and erect and primitive curiosity, and with unwearied gizzard, whose corrugations even yet need no sharpening, just as some little four-year-old bencher his two-cent gilt-covered edition of Cinderella, — without any improvement, that I can see, in the pronunciation, or accent, or emphasis, or any more skill in extracting or inserting the moral. The result is dulness of sight, a stagnation of the vital circulations, and a general deliquium and sloughing off of all the intellectual faculties. This sort of gingerbread is baked daily and more sedulously than pure wheat or rye-and-Indian in almost every oven, and finds a surer market.

The best books are not read even by those who are called good readers. What does our Concord culture amount to? There is in this town, with a very few exceptions, no taste for the best or for very good books even in English literature, whose words all can read and spell. Even the college-bred and so called liberally educated men here and elsewhere have really little or no acquaintance with the English classics; and as for the recorded wisdom of mankind, the ancient classics and Bibles, which are accessible to all who will know of them, there are the feeblest efforts any where made to become acquainted with them. I know a woodchopper, of middle age, who takes a French paper, not for news as he says, for he is above that, but to "keep himself in practice," he being a Canadian by birth; and when I ask him what he considers the best thing he can do in this world, he says, beside this, to keep up and add to his English. This is about as much as the college bred generally do or aspire to do, and they take an English paper for the purpose. One who has just come from reading perhaps one of the best English books will find how many with whom he can converse about it? Or suppose he comes from reading a Greek or Latin classic in the original, whose praises are familiar even to the so called illiterate; he will find nobody at all to speak to, but must keep silence about it. Indeed, there is hardly the professor in our colleges, who, if he has mastered the difficulties of the language, has proportionally mastered the difficulties of the wit and poetry of a Greek poet, and has any sympathy to impart to the alert and heroic reader; and as for the sacred Scriptures, or Bibles of mankind, who in this town can tell me even their titles? Most men do not know that any nation but the Hebrews have had a scripture. A man, any man, will go considerably out of his way to pick up a silver dollar; but here are golden words, which the wisest men of antiquity have uttered, and whose worth the wise of every succeeding age have assured us of; — and yet we learn to read only as far as Easy Reading, the primers and class-books, and when we leave school, the "Little Reading," and story books, which are for boys and beginners; and our reading, our conversation and thinking, are all on a very low level, worthy only of pygmies and manikins.

I aspire to be acquainted with wiser men than this our Concord soil has produced, whose names are hardly known here. Or shall I hear the name of Plato and never read his book? As if Plato were my townsman and I never saw him, — my next neighbor and I never heard him speak or attended to the wisdom of his words. But how actually is it? His Dialogues, which contain what was immortal in him, lie on the next shelf, and yet I never read them. We are under-bred and low-lived and illiterate; and in this respect I confess I do not make any very broad distinction between the illiterateness of my townsman who cannot read at all, and the illiterateness of him who has learned to read only what is for children and feeble intellects. We should be as good as the worthies of antiquity, but partly by first knowing how good they were. We are a race of tit-men, and soar but little higher in our intellectual flights than the columns of the daily paper.

It is not all books that are as dull as their readers. There are probably words addressed to our condition exactly, which, if we could really hear and understand, would be more salutary than the morning or the spring to our lives, and possibly put a new aspect on the face of things for us. How many a man has dated a new era in his life from the reading of a book! The book exists for us perchance which will explain our miracles and reveal new ones. The at present unutterable things we may find somewhere uttered. These same questions that disturb and puzzle and confound us have in their turn occurred to all the wise men; not one has been omitted; and each has answered them, according to his ability, by his words and his life. Moreover, with wisdom we shall learn liberality. The solitary hired man on a farm in the outskirts of Concord, who has had his second birth and peculiar religious experience, and is driven as he believes into silent gravity and exclusiveness by his faith, may think it is not true; but Zoroaster, thousands of years ago, travelled the same road and had the same experience; but he, being wise, knew it to be universal, and treated his neighbors accordingly, and is even said to have invented and established worship among men. Let him humbly commune with Zoroaster then, and, through the liberalizing influence of all the worthies, with Jesus Christ himself, and let "our church" go by the board.

We boast that we belong to the nineteenth century and are making the most rapid strides of any nation. But consider how little this village does for its own culture. I do not wish to flatter my townsmen, nor to be flattered by them, for that will not advance either of us. We need to be provoked, —

goaded like oxen, as we are, into a trot. We have a comparatively decent
system of common schools, schools for infants only; but excepting the
half-starved Lyceum in the winter, and latterly the puny beginning of a
library suggested by the state, no school for ourselves. We spend more on
almost any article of bodily aliment or ailment than on our mental aliment.
It is time that we had uncommon schools, that we did not leave off our
education when we begin to be men and women. It is time that villages
were universities, and their elder inhabitants the fellows of universities,
with leisure — if they are indeed so well off — to pursue liberal studies the
rest of their lives. Shall the world be confined to one Paris or one Oxford
forever? Cannot students be boarded here and get a liberal education under
the skies of Concord? Can we not hire some Abelard to lecture to us? Alas!
what with foddering the cattle and tending the store, we are kept from
school too long, and our education is sadly neglected. In this country, the
village should in some respects take the place of the nobleman of Europe.
It should be the patron of the fine arts. It is rich enough. It wants only the
magnanimity and refinement. It can spend money enough on such things
as farmers and traders value, but it is thought Utopian to propose spending
money for things which more intelligent men know to be of far more worth.
This town has spent seventeen thousand dollars on a town-house, thank
fortune or politics, but probably it will not spend so much on living wit,
the true meat to put into that shell, in a hundred years. The one hundred
and twenty-five dollars annually subscribed for a Lyceum in the winter
is better spent than any other equal sum raised in the town. If we live in
the nineteenth century, why should we not enjoy the advantages which the
nineteenth century offers? Why should our life be in any respect provincial?
If we will read newspapers, why not skip the gossip of Boston and take the
best newspaper in the world at once? — not be sucking the pap of "neutral
family" papers, or browsing "Olive-Branches" here in New England. Let
the reports of all the learned societies come to us, and we will see if they
know any thing. Why should we leave it to Harper & Brothers and Redding
& Co. to select our reading? As the nobleman of cultivated taste surrounds
himself with whatever conduces to his culture, — genius — learning — wit
— books — paintings — statuary — music — philosophical instruments,
and the like; so let the village do, — not stop short at a pedagogue, a
parson, a sexton, a parish library, and three selectmen, because our pilgrim
forefathers got through a cold winter once on a bleak rock with these. To act
collectively is according to the spirit of our institutions; and I am confident
that, as our circumstances are more flourishing, our means are greater than
the nobleman's. New England can hire all the wise men in the world to
come and teach her, and board them round the while, and not be provincial
at all. That is the uncommon school we want. Instead of noblemen, let us

have noble villages of men. If it is necessary, omit one bridge over the river, go round a little there, and throw one arch at least over the darker gulf of ignorance which surrounds us.

2
On the Ignorance of the Learned

by William Hazlitt

For the more languages a man can speak,
His talent has but sprung the greater leak:
And, for the industry he has spent upon't,
Must full as much some other way discount.
The Hebrew, Chaldee, and the Syriac
Do, like their letters, set men's reason back,
And turn their wits that strive to understand It
(Like those that write the characters) left-handed.
Yet he that is but able to express
No sense at all in several languages
Will pass for learneder than he that's known
To speak the strongest reason in his own.
– Samule Butler

The description of persons who have the fewest ideas of all others are mere authors and readers. It is better to be able neither to read nor write than to be able to do nothing else. A lounger who is ordinarily seen with a book in his hand is (we may be almost sure) equally without the power or inclination to attend either to what passes around him or in his own mind. Such a one may be said to carry his understanding about with him in his pocket, or to leave it at home on his library shelves. He is afraid of venturing on any train of reasoning, or of striking out any observation that is not mechanically suggested to him by parsing his eyes over certain legible characters; shrinks from the fatigue of thought, which, for want of practice, becomes insupportable to him; and sits down contented with an endless, wearisome succession of words and half-formed images, which fill the void of the mind, and continually efface one another. Learning is, in too many cases, but a foil to common sense; a substitute for true knowledge. Books are less often made use of as 'spectacles' to look at nature with, than as blinds to keep out its strong light and shifting scenery from weak eyes and indolent dispositions. The book-worm wraps himself up in his web of verbal generalities, and sees only the glimmering shadows of things reflected from the minds of others. Nature *puts him out.* The impressions of real objects, stripped of the disguises of words and voluminous roundabout descriptions, are blows that stagger him; their variety distracts, their rapidity exhausts him; and he turns from the bustle, the noise, and glare, and whirling motion of the world about him (which he has not an eye to follow in its fantastic changes, nor an understanding to reduce to fixed principles), to the quiet monotony of the dead languages, and the less startling and more intelligible combinations of the letters of the alphabet. It is well, it is perfectly well. 'Leave me to my repose,' is the motto of the sleeping and the dead. You might as well ask the paralytic to leap from his chair and throw away his crutch, or, without a miracle, to 'take up his bed and walk,' as expect the learned reader to throw down his book and think for himself. He clings to it for his intellectual support; and his dread of being left to himself is like the horror of a vacuum. He can only breathe a learned atmosphere, as other men breathe common air. He is a borrower of sense. He has no ideas of his own, and must live on those of other people. The habit of supplying our ideas from foreign sources 'enfeebles all internal strength of thought,' as a course of dram-drinking destroys the tone of the stomach. The faculties of the mind, when not exerted, or when cramped by custom and authority, become listless, torpid, and unfit for the purposes of thought or action. Can we wonder at the languor and lassitude which is thus produced by a life of learned sloth and ignorance; by poring over lines and syllables that excite little more idea or interest than if they were the characters of an unknown tongue, till the eye closes on vacancy, and the book drops from the feeble hand! I would rather be a wood-cutter, or the meanest hind, that all day 'sweats in the eye of Phoebus, and at night sleeps in Elysium,' than wear out my life so, 'twixt dreaming and awake.' The learned author differs from the learned student in this, that the one transcribes what the other reads. The learned are mere literary drudges. If you set them upon original composition, their heads turn, they don't know where they are. The indefatigable readers of books are like the everlasting copiers of pictures, who, when they attempt to do anything of their own, find they want an eye quick enough, a hand steady enough, and colours bright enough, to trace the living forms of nature.

Any one who has passed through the regular gradations of a classical education, and is not made a fool by it, may consider himself as having had a very narrow escape. It is an old remark, that boys who shine at school do not make the greatest figure when they grow up and come out into the world. The things, in fact, which a boy is set to learn at school, and on which his success depends, are things which do not require the exercise either of the highest or the most useful faculties of the mind. Memory (and that of the lowest kind) is the chief faculty called into play in conning over and repeating lessons by rote in grammar, in languages, in geography, arithmetic, etc., so that he who has the most of this technical memory, with the least turn for other things, which have a stronger and more natural claim upon his childish attention, will make the most forward school-boy. The jargon containing the definitions of the parts of speech, the rules for casting up an account, or the inflections of a Greek verb, can have no attraction to the tyro of ten years old, except as they are imposed as a task upon him by others, or from his feeling the want of sufficient relish of amusement in other things. A lad with a sickly constitution and no very active mind, who can just retain what is pointed out to him, and has neither sagacity to distinguish nor spirit to enjoy for himself, will generally be at the head of his form. An idler at school, on the other hand, is one who has high health and spirits, who has the free use of his limbs, with all his wits about him, who feels the circulation of his blood and the motion of his heart, who is ready to laugh and cry in a breath, and who had rather chase a ball or a butterfly, feel the open air in his face, look at the fields or the sky, follow a winding path, or enter with eagerness into all the little conflicts and interests of his acquaintances and friends, than doze over a musty spelling-book, repeat barbarous distichs after his master, sit so many hours pinioned to a writing-desk, and receive his reward for the loss of time and pleasure in paltry prize-medals at Christmas and Midsummer. There is indeed a degree of stupidity which prevents children from learning the usual lessons, or ever arriving at these puny academic honours. But what passes for stupidity is much oftener a want of interest, of a sufficient motive to fix the attention and force a reluctant application to the dry and unmeaning pursuits of school-learning. The best capacities are as much above this drudgery as the dullest are beneath it. Our men of the greatest genius have not been most distinguished for their acquirements at school or at the university.

Th' enthusiast Fancy was a truant ever.

Gray and Collins were among the instances of this wayward disposition. Such persons do not think so highly of the advantages, nor can they submit their imaginations so servilely to the trammels of strict scholastic discipline. There is a certain kind and degree of intellect in which words take root, but into which things have not power to penetrate. A mediocrity of talent, with a certain slenderness of moral constitution, is the soil that produces the most brilliant specimens of successful prize-essayists and Greek epigrammatists. It should not be forgotten that the least respectable character among modern politicians was the cleverest boy at Eton.

Learning is the knowledge of that which is not generally known to others, and which we can only derive at second-hand from books or other artificial sources. The knowledge of that which is before us, or about us, which appeals to our experience, passions, and pursuits, to the bosoms and businesses of men, is not learning. Learning is the knowledge of that which none but the learned know. He is the most learned man who knows the most of what is farthest removed from common life and actual observation, that is of the least practical utility, and least liable to be brought to the test of experience, and that, having been handed down through the greatest number of intermediate stages, is the most full of uncertainty, difficulties, and contradictions. It is seeing with the eyes of others, hearing with their ears, and pinning our faith on their understandings. The learned man prides himself in the knowledge of names and dates, not of men or things. He thinks and cares nothing about his next-door neighbours, but he is deeply read in the tribes and castes of the Hindoos and Calmue Tartars. He can hardly find his way into the next street, though he is acquainted with the exact dimensions of Constantinople and Pekin. He does not know whether his oldest acquaintance is a knave or a fool, but he can pronounce a pompous lecture on all the principal characters in history. He cannot tell whether an object is black or white, round or square, and yet he is a professed master of the laws of optics and the rules of perspective. He knows as much of what he talks about as a blind man does of colours. He cannot give a satisfactory answer to the plainest question, nor is he ever in the right in any one of his opinions upon any one matter of fact that really comes before him, and yet he gives himself out for an infallible judge on all these points, of which it is impossible that he or any other person living should know anything but by conjecture. He is expert in all the dead and in most of the living languages; but he can neither speak his own fluently, nor write it correctly. A person of this class, the second Greek scholar of his day, undertook to point out several solecisms in Milton's Latin style; and in his own performance there is hardly a sentence of common English. Such was Dr. — . Such is Dr. —. Such was not Porson. He was an exception that confirmed the general rule, a man that, by uniting talents and knowledge with learning, made the distinction between them more striking and palpable.

A mere scholar, who knows nothing but books, must be ignorant even of them. 'Books do not teach the use of books.' How should he know anything of a work who knows nothing of the subject of it? The learned pedant is conversant with books only as they are made of other books, and those again of others, without end. He parrots those who have parroted others. He can translate the same word into ten different languages, but he knows nothing of the *thing* which it means in any one of them. He stuffs his head with authorities built on authorities, with quotations quoted from quotations, while he locks up his senses, his understanding, and his heart. He is unacquainted with the maxims and manners of the world; he is to seek in the characters of individuals. He sees no beauty in the face of nature or of art. To him 'the mighty world of eye and ear' is hid; and 'knowledge,' except at one entrance, 'quite shut out.' His pride takes part with his ignorance; and his self-importance rises with the number of things of which be does not know the value, and which he therefore despises as unworthy of his notice. He knows nothing of pictures,—'Of the colouring of Titian, the grace of Raphael, the purity of Domenichino, the *corregioscity* of Correggio, the learning of Poussin, the airs of Guido, the taste of the Caracci, or the grand contour of Michael Angelo,'—of all those glories of the Italian and miracles of the Flemish school, which have filled the eyes of mankind with delight, and to the study and imitation of which thousands have in vain devoted their lives. These are to him as if they had never been, a mere dead letter, a by-word; and no wonder, for he neither sees nor understands their prototypes in nature. A print of Rubens' Watering-place or Claude's Enchanted Castle may be hanging on the walls of his room for months without his once perceiving them; and if you point them out to him he will turn away from them. The language of nature, or of art (which is another nature), is one that he does not understand. He repeats indeed the names of Apelles and Phidias, because they are to be found in classic authors, and boasts of their works as prodigies, because they no longer exist; or when he sees the finest remains of Grecian art actually before him in the Elgin Marbles, takes no other interest in them than as they lead to a learned dispute, and (which is the same thing) a quarrel about the meaning of a Greek particle. He is equally ignorant of music; he 'knows no touch of it,' from the strains of the all-accomplished Mozart to the shepherd's pipe upon the mountain. His ears are nailed to his books; and deadened with the sound of the Greek and Latin tongues, and the din and smithery of school-learning. Does he know anything more of poetry? He knows the number of feet in a verse, and of acts in a play; but of the soul or spirit he knows nothing. He can turn a Greek ode into English, or a Latin epigram into Greek verse; but whether either is worth the trouble he leaves to the critics. Does he understand 'the act and practique part of life' better than 'the theorique'? No. He knows no liberal or mechanic art, no trade or occupation, no game of skill or chance. Learning 'has no skill in surgery,' in agriculture, in building, in working in wood or in iron; it cannot make any instrument of labour, or use it when made; it cannot handle the plough or the spade, or the chisel or the hammer; it knows nothing of hunting or hawking, fishing or shooting, of horses or dogs, of fencing or dancing, or cudgel-playing, or bowls, or cards, or tennis, or anything else. The learned professor of all arts and sciences cannot reduce any one of them to practice, though he may contribute an account of them to an Encyclopedia. He has not the use of his hands nor of his feet; he can neither run, nor walk, nor swim; and he considers all those who actually understand and can exercise any of these arts of body or mind as vulgar and mechanical men,—though to know almost any one of them in perfection requires long time and practice, with powers originally fitted, and a turn of mind particularly devoted to them. It does not require more than this to enable the learned candidate to arrive, by painful study, at a doctor's degree and a fellowship, and to eat, drink, and sleep the rest of his life!

The thing is plain. All that men really understand is confined to a very small compass; to their daily affairs and experience; to what they have an opportunity to know, and motives to study or practise. The rest is affectation and imposture. The common people have the use of their limbs; for they live by their labour or skill. They understand their own business and the characters of those they have to deal with; for it is necessary that they should. They have eloquence to express their passions, and wit at will to express their contempt and provoke laughter. Their natural use of speech is not hung up in monumental mockery, in an obsolete language; nor is their sense of what is ludicrous, or readiness at finding out allusions to express it, buried in collections of *Anas.* You will hear more good things on the outside of a stage-coach from London to Oxford than if you were to pass a twelvemonth with the undergraduates, or heads of colleges, of that famous university; and more *home* truths are to be learnt from listening to a noisy debate in an alehouse than from attending a formal one in the House of Commons. An elderly country gentlewoman will often know more of character, and be able to illustrate it by more amusing anecdotes taken from the history of what has been said, done, and gossiped in a country town for the last fifty years, than the best bluestocking of the age will be able to glean from that sort of learning which consists in an acquaintance with all the novels and satirical poems published in the same period. People in towns, indeed, are woefully deficient in a knowledge of character, which they see only *in the bust,* not as a whole-length. People in the country not only know all that has happened to a man, but trace his virtues or vices, as they do his features, in their descent through several generations, and solve some contradiction in his behaviour by a cross in the breed half a century ago. The learned know nothing of the matter, either in town or country. Above all, the mass of society have common sense, which the learned in all ages want. The vulgar are in the right when they judge for themselves; they are wrong when they trust to their blind guides. The celebrated nonconformist divine, Baxter, was almost stoned to death by the good women of Kidderminster, for asserting from the pulpit that 'hell was paved with infants' skulls'; but, by the force of argument, and of learned quotations from the Fathers, the reverend preacher at length prevailed over the scruples of his congregation, and over reason and humanity.

Such is the use which has been made of human learning. The labourers in this vineyard seem as if it was their object to confound all common sense, and the distinctions of good and evil, by means of traditional maxims and preconceived notions taken upon trust, and increasing in absurdity with increase of age. They pile hypothesis on hypothesis, mountain high, till it is impossible to come at the plain truth on any question. They see things, not as they are, but as they find them in books, and 'wink and shut their apprehensions up,' in order that they may discover nothing to interfere with their prejudices or convince them of their absurdity. It might be supposed that the height of human wisdom consisted in maintaining contradictions and rendering nonsense sacred. There is no dogma, however fierce or foolish, to which these persons have not set their seals, and tried to impose on the understandings of their followers as the will of Heaven, clothed with all the terrors and sanctions of religion. How little has the human understanding been directed to find out the true and useful! How much ingenuity has been thrown away in the defence of creeds and systems! How much time and talents have been wasted in theological controversy, in law, in politics, in verbal criticism, in judicial astrology, and in finding out the art of making gold! What actual benefit do we reap from the writings of a Laud or a Whitgift, or of Bishop Bull or Bishop Waterland, or Prideaux' Connections, or Beausobre, or Calmet, or St. Augustine, or Puffendord, or Vattel, or from the more literal but equally learned and unprofitable labours of Scaliger, Cardan, and Scioppius? How many grains of sense are there in their thousand folio or quarto volumes? What would the world lose if they were committed to the flames to-morrow? Or are they not already 'gone to the vault of all the Capulets'? Yet all these were oracles in their time, and would have scoffed at you or me, at common sense and human nature, for differing with them. It is our turn to laugh now.

To conclude this subject. The most sensible people to be met with in society are men of business and of the world, who argue from what they see and know, instead of spinning cobweb distinctions of what things ought to be. Women have often more of what is called *good sense* than men. They have fewer pretensions; are less implicated in theories; and judge of objects more from their immediate and involuntary impression on the mind, and, therefore, more truly and naturally. They cannot reason wrong; for they do not reason at all. They do not think or speak by rule; and they have in general more eloquence and wit, as well as sense, on that account. By their wit, sense, and eloquence together, they generally contrive to govern their husbands. Their style, when they write to their friends (not for the booksellers), is better than that of most authors.—Uneducated people have most exuberance of invention and the greatest freedom from prejudice. Shakespear's was evidently an uneducated mind, both in the freshness of his imagination and in the variety of his views; as Milton's was scholastic, in the texture both of his thoughts and feelings. Shakespear had not been accustomed to write themes at school in favour of virtue or against vice. To this we owe the unaffected but healthy tone of his dramatic morality. If we wish to know the force of human genius we should read Shakespear. If we wish to see the insignificance of human learning we may study his commentators.

3
What is a Classic?

by Charles-Augustin Sainte-Beuve

A delicate question, to which somewhat diverse solutions might be given according to times and seasons. An intelligent man suggests it to me, and I intend to try, if not to solve it, at least to examine and discuss it face to face with my readers, were it only to persuade them to answer it for themselves, and, if I can, to make their opinion and mine on the point clear. And why, in criticism, should we not, from time to time, venture to treat some of those subjects which are not personal, in which we no longer speak of some one but of some thing? Our neighbours, the English, have well succeeded in making of it a special division of literature under the modest title of "Essays." It is true that in writing of such subjects, always slightly abstract and moral, it is advisable to speak of them in a season of quiet, to make sure of our own attention and of that of others, to seize one of those moments of calm moderation and leisure seldom granted our amiable France; even when she is desirous of being wise and is not making revolutions, her brilliant genius can scarcely tolerate them.

A classic, according to the usual definition, is an old author canonised by admiration, and an authority in his particular style. The word classic was first used in this sense by the Romans. With them not all the citizens of the different classes were properly called *classici,* but only those of the chief class, those who possessed an income of a certain fixed sum. Those who possessed a smaller income were described by the term *infra classem,* below the preeminent class. The word *classicus* was used in a figurative sense by Aulus Gellius, and applied to writers: a writer of worth and distinction, *classicus assiduusque scriptor,* a writer who is of account, has real property, and is not lost in the proletariate crowd. Such an expression implies an age sufficiently advanced to have already made some sort of valuation and classification of literature.

At first the only true classics for the moderns were the ancients.

The Greeks, by peculiar good fortune and natural enlightenment of mind, had no classics but themselves. They were at first the only classical authors for the Romans, who strove and contrived to imitate them. After the great periods of Roman literature, after Cicero and Virgil, the Romans in their turn had their classics, who became almost exclusively the classical authors of the centuries which followed. The middle ages, which were less ignorant of Latin antiquity than is believed, but which lacked proportion and taste, confused the ranks and orders. Ovid was placed above Homer, and Boetius seemed a classic equal to Plato. The revival of learning in the fifteenth and sixteenth centuries helped to bring this long chaos to order, and then only was admiration rightly proportioned. Thenceforth the true classical authors of Greek and Latin antiquity stood out in a luminous background, and were harmoniously grouped on their two heights.

Meanwhile modern literatures were born, and some of the more precocious, like the Italian, already possessed the style of antiquity. Dante appeared, and, from the very first, posterity greeted him as a classic. Italian poetry has since shrunk into far narrower bounds; but, whenever it desired to do so, it always found again and preserved the impulse and echo of its lofty origin. It is no indifferent matter for a poetry to derive its point of departure and classical source in high places; for example, to spring from Dante rather than to issue laboriously from Malherbe.

Modern Italy had her classical authors, and Spain had every right to believe that she also had hers at a time when France was yet seeking hers. A few talented writers endowed with originality and exceptional animation, a few brilliant efforts, isolated, without following, interrupted and recommenced, did not suffice to endow a nation with a solid and imposing basis of literary wealth. The idea of a *classic* implies something that has continuance and consistency, which forms a unity and makes a tradition, which transmits itself to posterity, and endures. It was only after the glorious years of Louis XIV. that the nation felt with tremor and pride that such good fortune had happened to her. Every voice informed Louis XIV. of it with flattery, exaggeration, and emphasis, yet with a certain sentiment of truth. Then arose a singular and striking contradiction: those men of whom Perrauit was the chief, the men who were most smitten with the marvels of the age of Louis the Great, who even went the length of sacrificing the ancients to the moderns, aimed at exalting and canonising even those whom they regarded as inveterate opponents and adversaries. Boileau avenged and angrily upheld the ancients against Perrault, who extolled the moderns— that is to say, Corneille, Moliere, Pascal, and the eminent men of his age, Boileau, one of the first, included. Kindly La Fontaine, taking part in the dispute in behalf of the learned Huet, did not perceive that, in spite of his defects, he was in his turn on the point of being held as a classic himself.

Example is the best definition. From the time France possessed her age of Louis XIV. and could contemplate it at a little distance, she knew, better than by any arguments, what to be classical meant. The eighteenth century, even in its medley of things, strengthened this idea through some fine works, due to its four great men. Read Voltaire's *Age of Louis XIV.,* Montesquieu's

Greatness and Fall of the Romans, Buffon's *Epochs of Nature,* the beautiful pages of reverie and natural description of Rousseau's *Savoyard Vicar,* and say if the eighteenth century, in these memorable works, did not understand how to reconcile tradition with freedom of development and independence. But at the be ginning of the present century and under the Empire, in sight of the first attempts of a decidedly new and somewhat adventurous literature, the idea of a classic in a few resisting minds, more sorrowful than severe, was strangely narrowed and contracted. The first *Dictionary of the Academy* (1694) merely defined a classical author as "a much-approved ancient writer, who is an authority as regards the subject he treats." The *Dictionary of the Academy* of 1835 narrows that definition still more, and gives precision and even limit to its rather vague form. It describes classical authors as those "who have become models in any language whatever," and in all the articles which follow, the expressions, models, fixed rules for composition and style, strict rules of art to which men must conform, continually recur. That definition of classic was evidently made by the respectable Academicians, our predecessors, in face and sight of what was then called romantic—that is to say, in sight of the enemy. It seems to me time to renounce those timid and restrictive definitions and to free our mind of them. A true classic, as I should like to hear it defined, is an author who has enriched the human mind, increased its treasure, and caused it to advance a step; who has discovered some moral and not equivocal truth, or revealed some eternal passion in that heart where all seemed known and discovered; who has expressed his thought, observation, or invention, in no matter what form, only provided it be broad and great, refined and sensible, sane and beautiful in itself; who has spoken to all in his own peculiar style, a style which is found to be also that of the whole world, a style new without neologism, new and old, easily contemporary with all time.

Such a classic may for a moment have been revolutionary; it may at least have seemed so, but it is not; it only lashed and subverted whatever prevented the restoration of the balance of order and beauty.

If it is desired, names may be applied to this definition which I wish to make purposely majestic and fluctuating, or in a word, all-embracing. I should first put there Corneille of the *Polyeucte,* Cinna, and Horaces. I should put Moliere there, the fullest and most complete poetic genius we have ever had in France. Goethe, the king of critics, said: —

"Moliere is so great that he astonishes us afresh every time we read him. He is a man apart; his plays border on the tragic, and no one has the courage to try and imitate him. His *Avare,* where vice destroys all affection between father and son, is one of the most sublime works, and dramatic in the highest degree. In a drama every action ought to be important in itself, and to lead to an action greater still. In this respect *Tartuffe* is a model. What a piece of exposition the first scene is! From the beginning everything has an important meaning, and causes something much more important to be foreseen. The exposition in a certain play of Lessing that might be mentioned is very fine, but the world only sees that of *Tartuffe* once. It is the finest of the kind we possess. Every year I read a play of Moliere, just as from time to time I contemplate some engraving after the great Italian masters."

I do not conceal from myself that the definition of the classic I have just given somewhat exceeds the notion usually ascribed to the term. It should, above all, include conditions of uniformity, wisdom, moderation, and reason, which dominate and contain all the others. Having to praise M. Royer-Collard, M. de Remusat said—"If he derives purity of taste, propriety of terms, variety of expression, attentive care in suiting the diction to the thought, from our classics, he owes to himself alone the distinctive character he gives it all." It is here evident that the part allotted to classical qualities seems mostly to depend on harmony and nuances of expression, on graceful and temperate style: such is also the most general opinion. In this sense the pre-eminent classics would be writers of a middling order, exact, sensible, elegant, always clear, yet of noble feeling and airily veiled strength. Marie-Joseph Chenier has described the poetics of those temperate and accomplished writers in lines where he shows himself their happy disciple:—

"It is good sense, reason which does all,—virtue, genius, soul, talent, and taste.—What is virtue? reason put in practice;—talent? reason expressed with brilliance;—soul? reason delicately put forth;—and genius is sublime reason."

While writing those lines he was evidently thinking of Pope, Boileau, and Horace, the master of them all. The peculiar characteristic of the theory which subordinated imagination and feeling itself to reason, of which Scaliger perhaps gave the first sign among the moderns, is, properly speaking, the Latin theory, and for a long time it was also by preference the French theory. If it is used appositely, if the term reason is not abused, that theory possesses some truth; but it is evident that it is abused, and that if, for instance, reason can be confounded with poetic genius and make one with it in a moral epistle, it cannot be the same thing as the genius, so varied and so diversely creative in its expression of the passions, of the drama or the epic. Where will you find reason in the fourth book of the Aeneid and the transports of Dido? Be that as it may, the spirit which prompted the theory, caused writers who ruled their inspiration, rather than those who abandoned themselves to it, to be placed in the first rank of classics; to put

Virgil there more surely than Homer, Racine in preference to Corneille. The masterpiece to which the theory likes to point, which in fact brings together all conditions of prudence, strength, tempered boldness, moral elevation, and grandeur, is *Athalie.* Turenne in his two last campaigns and Racine in *Athalie* are the great examples of what wise and prudent men are capable of when they reach the maturity of their genius and attain their supremest boldness.

Buffon, in his *Discourse on Style,* insisting on the unity of design, arrangement, and execution, which are the stamps of true classical works, said:—"Every subject is one, and however vast it is, it can be comprised in a single treatise. Interruptions, pauses, sub-divisions should only be used when many subjects are treated, when, having to speak of great, intricate, and dissimilar things, the march of genius is interrupted by the multiplicity of obstacles, and contracted by the necessity of circumstances: otherwise, far from making a work more solid, a great number of divisions destroys the unity of its parts; the book appears clearer to the view, but the author's design remains obscure." And he continues his criticism, having in view Montesquieu's *Spirit of Laws,* an excellent book at bottom, but sub-divided: the famous author, worn out before the end, was unable to infuse inspiration into all his ideas, and to arrange all his matter. However, I can scarcely believe that Buffon was not also thinking, by way of contrast, of Bossuet's *Discourse on Universal History,* a subject vast indeed, and yet of such an unity that the great orator was able to comprise it in a single treatise. When we open the first edition, that of 1681, before the division into chapters, which was introduced later, passed from the margin into the text, very thing is developed in a single series, almost in one breath. It might be said that the orator has here acted like the nature of which Buffon speaks, that "he has worked on an eternal plan from which he has nowhere departed," so deeply does he seem to have entered into the familiar counsels and designs of providence.

Are *Athalie* and the *Discourse on Universal History* the greatest masterpieces that the strict classical theory can present to its friends as well as to its enemies? In spite of the admirable simplicity and dignity in the achievement of such unique productions, we should like, nevertheless, in the interests of art, to expand that theory a little, and to show that it is possible to enlarge it without relaxing the tension. Goethe, whom I like to quote on such a subject, said:—

"I call the classical healthy, and the romantic sickly. In my opinion the Nibelungen song is as much a classic as Homer. Both are healthy and vigorous. The works of the day are romantic, not because they are new, but because they are weak, ailing, or sickly. Ancient works are classical not because they are old, but because they are powerful, fresh, and healthy. If we regarded romantic and classical from those two points of view we should soon all agree."

Indeed, before determining and fixing the opinions on that matter, I should like every unbiassed mind to take a voyage round the world and devote itself to a survey of different literatures in their primitive vigour and infinite variety. What would be seen? Chief of all a Homer, the father of the classical world, less a single distinct individual than the vast living expression of a whole epoch and a semi-barbarous civilisation. In order to make him a true classic, it was necessary to attribute to him later a design, a plan, literary invention, qualities of atticism and urbanity of which he had certainly never dreamed in the luxuriant development of his natural inspirations. And who appear by his side? August, venerable ancients, the Aeschyluses and the Sophocles, mutilated, it is true, and only there to present us with a debris of themselves, the survivors of many others as worthy, doubtless, as they to survive, but who have succumbed to the injuries of time. This thought alone would teach a man of impartial mind not to look upon the whole of even classical literatures with a too narrow and restricted view; he would learn that the exact and well-proportioned order which has since so largely prevailed in our admiration of the past was only the outcome of artificial circumstances.

And in reaching the modern world, how would it be? The greatest names to be seen at the beginning of literatures are those which disturb and run counter to certain fixed ideas of what is beautiful and appropriate in poetry. For example, is Shakespeare a classic? Yes, now, for England and the world; but in the time of Pope he was not considered so. Pope and his friends were the only pre-eminent classics; directly after their death they seemed so for ever. At the present time they are still classics, as they deserve to be, but they are only of the second order, and are for ever subordinated and relegated to their rightful place by him who has again come to his own on the height of the horizon.

It is not, however, for me to speak ill of Pope or his great disciples, above all, when they possess pathos and naturalness like Goldsmith: after the greatest they are perhaps the most agreeable writers and the poets best fitted to add charm to life. Once when Lord Bolingbroke was writing to Swift, Pope added a postscript, in which he said—"I think some advantage would result to our age, if we three spent three years together." Men who, without boasting, have the right to say such things must never be spoken of lightly: the fortunate ages, when men of talent could propose such things, then no chimera, are rather to be envied. The ages called by the name of Louis XIV. or of Queen Anne are, in the dispassionate sense of the word, the only true classical ages, those which offer protection and a favourable climate to real talent. We know only to well how in our untrammelled times, through the instability and storminess of the age, talents are lost and dissipated. Nevertheless, let us acknowledge our age's part and superiority in greatness. True and sovereign genius triumphs over the very difficulties that cause others to fail: Dante, Shakespeare, and Milton were able to attain their height and produce their imperishable works in spite of obstacles, hardships and tempests. Byron's opinion of Pope has been much discussed, and the explanation of it sought in the kind of contradiction by which the singer of *Don Juan* and *Childe Harold* extolled the purely classical school and pronounced it the only good one, while himself acting so differently. Goethe spoke the truth on that point when he remarked that Byron, great by the flow and source of poetry, feared that Shakespeare was more powerful than himself in the creation and realisation of his characters. "He would have liked to deny it; the elevation so free from egoism irritated him; he felt when near it that he could not display himself at ease. He never denied Pope, because he did not fear him; he knew that Pope was only a low wall by his side."

If, as Byron desired, Pope's school had kept the supremacy and a sort of honorary empire in the past, Byron would have been the first and only poet in his particular style; the height of Pope's wall shuts out Shakespeare's great figure from sight, whereas when Shakespeare reigns and rules in all his greatness, Byron is only second.

In France there was no great classic before the age of Louis XIV.; the Dantes and Shakespeares, the early authorities to whom, in times of emancipation, men sooner or later return, were wanting. There were mere sketches of great poets, like Mathurin Regnier, like Rabelais, without any ideal, without the depth of emotion and the seriousness which canonises. Montaigne was a kind of premature classic, of the family of Horace, but for want of worthy surroundings, like a spoiled child, he gave himself up to the unbridled fancies of his style and humour. Hence it happened that France, less than any other nation, found in her old authors a right to demand vehemently at a certain time literary liberty and freedom, and that it was more difficult for her, in enfranchising herself, to remain classical. However, with Moliere and La Fontaine among her classics of the great period, nothing could justly be refused to those who possessed courage and ability.

The important point now seems to me to be to uphold, while extending, the idea and belief. There is no recipe for making classics; this point should be clearly recognised. To believe that an author will become a classic by imitating certain qualities of purity, moderation, accuracy, and elegance, independently of the style and inspiration, is to believe that after Racine the father there is a place for Racine the son; dull and estimable role, the worst in poetry. Further, it is hazardous to take too quickly and without opposition the place of a classic in the sight of one's contemporaries; in that case there is a good chance of not retaining the position with posterity. Fontanes in his day was regarded by his friends as a pure classic; see how at twenty-five years' distance his star has set. How many of these precocious classics are there who do not endure, and who are so only for a while! We turn round one morning and are surprised not to find them standing behind us. Madame de Sevigne would wittily say they possessed but an evanescent colour. With regard to classics, the least expected prove the best and greatest: seek them rather in the vigorous genius born immortal and flourishing for ever. Apparently the least classical of the four great poets of the age of Louis XIV. was Moliere; he was then applauded far more than he was esteemed; men took delight in him without understanding his worth. After him, La Fontaine seemed the least classical: observe after two centuries what is the result for both. Far above Boileau, even above Racine, are they not now unanimously considered to possess in the highest degree the characteristics of an all-embracing morality?

Meanwhile there is no question of sacrificing or depreciating anything. I believe the temple of taste is to be rebuilt; but its reconstruction is merely a matter of enlargement, so that it may become the home of all noble human beings, of all who have permanently increased the sum of the mind's delights and possessions. As for me, who cannot, obviously, in any degree pretend to be the architect or designer of such a temple, I shall confine myself to expressing a few earnest wishes, to submit, as it were, my designs for the edifice. Above all I should desire not to exclude any one among the worthy, each should be in his place there, from Shakespeare, the freest of creative geniuses, and the greatest of classics without knowing it, to Andrieux, the last of classics in miniature. "In my Father's house are many mansions;" that should be as true of the kingdom of the beautiful here below, as of the kingdom of Heaven. Homer, as always and everywhere, should be first, likest a god; but behind him, like the procession of the three wise kings of the East, would be seen the three great poets, the three Homers, so long ignored by us, who wrote epics for the use of the old peoples of Asia, the poets Valmiki, Vyasa of the Hindoos, and Firdousi of the Persians: in the domain of taste it is well to know that such men exist, and not to divide the human race. Our homage paid to what is recognized as soon as perceived, we must not stray further; the eye should delight in a thousand pleasing or majestic spectacles, should rejoice in a thousand varied and surprising combinations, whose apparent confusion would never be without concord and harmony.

The oldest of the wise men and poets, those who put human morality into maxims, and those who in simple fashion sung it, would converse together in rare and gentle speech, and would not be surprised at understanding each other's meaning at the very first word. Solon, Hesiod, Theognis, Job, Solomon, and why not Confucius, would welcome the cleverest moderns, La Rochefoucauld and La Bruyere, who, when listening to them, would say "they knew all that we know, and in repeating life's experiences, we have discovered nothing." On the hill, most easily discernible, and of most accessible ascent, Virgil, surrounded by Menander, Tibullus, Terence, Fenelon, would occupy himself in discoursing with them with great charm and divine enchantment: his gentle countenance would shine with an inner light, and be tinged with modesty; as on the day when entering the theatre at Rome, just as they finished reciting his verses, he saw the people rise with an unanimous movement and pay to him the same homage as to Augustus. Not far from him, regretting the separation from so dear a friend, Horace, in his turn, would preside (as far as so accomplished and wise a poet could preside) over the group of poets of social life who could talk although they sang,—Pope, Boileau, the one become less irritable, the other less fault-finding. Montaigne, a true poet, would be among them, and would give the finishing touch that should deprive that delightful corner of the air of a literary school. There would La Fontaine forget himself, and becoming less volatile would wander no more. Voltaire would be attracted by it, but while finding pleasure in it would not have patience to remain. A little lower down, on the same hill as Virgil, Xenophon, with simple bearing, looking in no way like a general, but rather resembling a priest of the Muses, would be seen gathering round him the Attics of every tongue and of every nation, the Addisons, Pellissons, Vauvenargues—all who feel the value of an easy persuasiveness, an exquisite simplicity, and a gentle negligence mingled with ornament. In the centre of the place, in the portico of the principal temple (for there would be several in the enclosure), three great men would like to meet often, and when they were together, no fourth, however great, would dream of joining their discourse or their silence. In them would be seen beauty, proportion in greatness, and that perfect harmony which appears but once in the full youth of the world. Their three names have become the ideal of art—Plato, Sophocles, and Demosthenes. Those demi-gods honoured, we see a numerous and familiar company of choice spirits who follow, the Cervantes and Molieres, practical painters of life, indulgent friends who are still the first of benefactors, who laughingly embrace all mankind, turn man's experience to gaiety, and know the powerful workings of a sensible, hearty, and legitimate joy. I do not wish to make this description, which if complete would fill a volume, any longer. In the middle ages, believe me, Dante would occupy the sacred heights: at the feet of the singer of Paradise all Italy would be spread out like a garden; Boccaccio and Ariosto would there disport themselves, and Tasso would find again the orange groves of Sorrento. Usually a corner would be reserved for each of the various nations, but the authors would take delight in leaving it, and in their travels would recognise, where we should least expect it, brothers or masters. Lucretius, for example, would enjoy discussing the origin of the world and the reducing of chaos to order with Milton. But both arguing from their own point of view, they would only agree as regards divine pictures of poetry and nature.

Such are our classics; each individual imagination may finish the sketch and choose the group preferred. For it is necessary to make a choice, and the first condition of taste, after obtaining knowledge of all, lies not in continual travel, but in rest and cessation from wandering. Nothing blunts and destroys taste so much as endless journeyings; the poetic spirit is not the Wandering Jew. However, when I speak of resting and making choice, my meaning is not that we are to imitate those who charm us most among our masters in the past. Let us be content to know them, to penetrate them, to admire them; but let us, the late-comers, endeavour to be ourselves. Let us have the sincerity and naturalness of our own thoughts, of our own feelings; so much is always possible. To that let us add what is more difficult, elevation, an aim, if possible, towards an exalted goal; and while speaking our own language, and submitting to the conditions of the times in which we live, whence we derive our strength and our defects, let us ask from time to time, our brows lifted towards the heights and our eyes fixed on the group of honoured mortals: what would that say of us?

But why speak always of authors and writings? Maybe an age is coming when there will be no more writing. Happy those who read and read again, those who in their reading can follow their unrestrained inclination! There comes a time in life when, all our journeys over, our experiences ended, there is no enjoyment more delightful than to study and thoroughly examine the things we know, to take pleasure in what we feel, and in seeing and seeing again the people we love: the pure joys of our maturity. Then it is that the word classic takes its true meaning, and is defined for every man of taste by an irresistible choice. Then taste is formed, it is shaped and definite; then good sense, if we are to possess it at all, is perfected in us. We have neither more time for experiments, nor a desire to go forth in search of newfound pastures. We cling to our friends, to those proved by long intercourse. Old wine, old books, old friends. We say to ourselves with Voltaire in these delightful lines:—"Let us enjoy, let us write, let us live, my dear Horace!...I have lived longer than you: my verse will not last so long. But on the brink of the tomb I shall make it my chief care—to follow the lessons of your philosophy—to despise death in enjoying life—to read your writings full of charm and good sense—as we drink an old wine which revives our senses."

In fact, be it Horace or another who is the author preferred, who reflects our thoughts in all the wealth of their maturity, of some one of those excellent and antique minds shall we request an interview at every moment; of some one of them shall we ask a friendship which never deceives, which could not fail us; to some one of them shall we appeal for that sensation of serenity and sweetness (we have often need of it) which reconciles us with mankind and with ourselves.

4
Of Kings' Treasuries

by John Ruskin

The first lecture says, or tries to say, that, life being very short, and the quiet hours of it few, we ought to waste none of them in reading valueless books; and that valuable books should, in a civilized country, be within the reach of every one, printed in excellent form, for a just price; but not in any vile, vulgar, or, by reason of smallness of type, physically injurious form, at a vile price. For we none of us need many books, and those which we need ought to be clearly printed, on the best paper, and strongly bound.

And though we are, indeed, now, a wretched and poverty-struck nation, and hardly able to keep soul and body together, still, as no person in decent circumstances would put on his table confessedly bad wine, or bad meat, without being ashamed, so he need not have on his shelves ill-printed or loosely and wretchedly-stitched books; for though few can be rich, yet every man who honestly exerts himself may, I think, still provide, for himself and his family, good shoes, good gloves, strong harness for his cart or carriage horses, and stout leather binding for his books. And I would urge upon every young man, as the beginning of his due and wise provision for his household, to obtain as soon as he can, by the severest economy, a restricted, serviceable, and steadily – however slowly – increasing, series of books for use through life; making his little library, of all the furniture in his room, the most studied and decorative piece; every volume having its assigned place, like a little statue in its niche, and one of the earliest and strictest lessons to the children of the house being how to turn the pages of their own literary possessions lightly and deliberately, with no chance of tearing or dog's ears.

§

My friends, I do not know why any of us should talk about reading. We want some sharper discipline than that of reading; but, at all events, be assured, we cannot read. No reading is possible for a people with its mind in this state. No sentence of any great writer is intelligible to them. It is simply and sternly impossible for the English public, at this moment, to understand any thoughtful writing,—so incapable of thought has it become in its insanity of avarice. Happily, our disease is, as yet, little worse than this incapacity of thought; it is not corruption of the inner nature; we ring true still, when anything strikes home to us; and though the idea that everything should "pay" has infected our every purpose so deeply, that even when we would play the good Samaritan, we never take out our two pence and give them to the host, without saying, "When I come again, thou shalt give me fourpence," there is a capacity of noble passion left in our hearts' core. We show it in our work—in our war,—even in those unjust domestic affections which make us furious at a small private wrong, while we are polite to a boundless public one: we are still industrious to the last hour of the day, though we add the gambler's fury to the labourer's patience; we are still brave to the death, though incapable of discerning true cause for battle; and are still true in affection to our own flesh, to the death, as the sea-monsters are, and the rock-eagles. And there is hope for a nation while this can be still said of it. As long as it holds its life in its hand, ready to give it for its honour (though a foolish honour), for its love (though a selfish love), and for its business (though a base business), there is hope for it. But hope only; for this instinctive, reckless virtue cannot last. No nation can last, which has made a mob of itself, however generous at heart. It must discipline its passions, and direct them, or they will discipline it, one day, with scorpion whips. Above all, a nation cannot last as a money-making mob: it cannot with impunity,—it cannot with existence,—go on despising literature, despising science, despising art, despising nature, despising compassion, and concentrating its soul on Pence. Do you think these are harsh or wild words? Have patience with me but a little longer. I will prove their truth to you, clause by clause.

I. I say first we have despised literature. What do we, as a nation, care about books? How much do you think we spend altogether on our libraries, public or private, as compared with what we spend on our horses? If a man spends lavishly on his library, you call him mad—a bibliomaniac. But you never call any one a horsemaniac, though men ruin themselves every day by their horses, and you do not hear of people ruining themselves by their books. Or, to go lower still, how much do you think the contents of the book-shelves of the United Kingdom, public and private, would fetch, as compared with the contents of its wine-cellars? What position would its expenditure on literature take, as compared with its expenditure on luxurious eating? We talk of food for the mind, as of food for the body: now a good book contains such food inexhaustibly; it is a provision for life, and for the best part of us; yet how long most people would look at the best book before they would give the price of a large turbot for it? Though there have been men who have pinched their stomachs and bared their backs to buy a book, whose libraries were cheaper to them, I think, in the end, than most men's dinners are. We are few of us put to such trial, and more the pity; for, indeed, a precious thing is all the more precious to us if it has been won by work or economy; and if public libraries were half so costly as public dinners, or books cost the tenth part of what bracelets do, even foolish men and women might sometimes suspect there was good in reading, as well as in munching and sparkling: whereas the very cheapness of literature is making even wise people forget that if a book is worth reading, it is worth buying. No book is worth anything which is not worth *much;* nor is it serviceable, until it has been read, and re-read, and loved, and loved again; and marked, so that you can refer to the passages you want in it, as a soldier can seize the weapon he needs in an armoury, or a housewife bring the spice she needs from her store. Bread of flour is good; but there is bread, sweet as honey, if we would eat it, in a good book; and the family must be poor indeed, which, once in their lives, cannot, for, such multipliable barley-loaves, pay their baker's bill. We call ourselves a rich nation, and we are filthy and foolish enough to thumb each other's books out of circulating libraries!

II. I say we have despised science. "What!" you exclaim, "are we not foremost in all discovery, {1} and is not the whole world giddy by reason, or unreason, of our inventions?" Yes; but do you suppose that is national work? That work is all done *in spite of* the nation; by private people's zeal and money. We are glad enough, indeed, to make our profit of science; we snap up anything in the way of a scientific bone that has meat on it, eagerly enough; but if the scientific man comes for a bone or a crust to *us,* that is another story. What have we publicly done for science? We are obliged to know what o'clock it is, for the safety of our ships, and therefore we pay for an observatory; and we allow ourselves, in the person of our Parliament, to be annually tormented into doing something, in a slovenly way, for the British Museum; sullenly apprehending that to be a place for keeping stuffed birds in, to amuse our children. If anybody will pay for their own telescope, and resolve another nebula, we cackle over the discernment as if it were our own; if one in ten thousand of our hunting squires suddenly perceives that the earth was indeed made to be something else than a portion for foxes, and burrows in it himself, and tells us where the gold is, and where the coals, we understand that there is some use in that; and very properly knight him: but is the accident of his having found out how to employ himself usefully any credit to *us?* (The negation of such discovery among his brother squires mayperhaps be some discredit to us, if we would consider of it.) But if you doubt these generalities, here is one fact for us all to meditate upon, illustrative of our love of science. Two years ago there was a collection of the fossils of Solenhofen to be sold in Bavaria; the best in existence, containing many specimens unique for perfectness, and one unique as an example of a species (a whole kingdom of unknown living creatures being announced by that fossil).

This collection, of which the mere market worth, among private buyers, would probably have been some thousand or twelve hundred pounds, was offered to the English nation for seven hundred: but we would not give seven hundred, and the whole series would have been in the Munich Museum at this moment, if Professor Owen {2} had not, with loss of his own time, and patient tormenting of the British public in person of its representatives, got leave to give four hundred pounds at once, and himself become answerable for the other three! which the said public will doubtless pay him eventually, but sulkily, and caring nothing about the matter all the while; only always ready to cackle if any credit comes of it. Consider, I beg of you, arithmetically, what this fact means. Your annual expenditure for public purposes, (a third of it for military apparatus,) is at least 50 millions. Now 700L. is to 50,000,000L. roughly, as seven pence to two thousand pounds. Suppose, then, a gentleman of unknown income, but whose wealth was to be conjectured from the fact that he spent two thousand a year on his park-walls and footmen only, professes himself fond of science; and that one of his servants comes eagerly to tell him that an unique collection of fossils, giving clue to a new era of creation, is to be had for the sum of seven pence sterling; and that the gentleman who is fond of science, and spends two thousand a year on his park, answers, after keeping his servant waiting several months, "Well! I'll give you fourpence for them, if you will be answerable for the extra threepence yourself, till next year!"

III. I say you have despised Art! "What!" you again answer, "have we not Art exhibitions, miles long? and do we not pay thousands of pounds for single pictures? and have we not Art schools and institutions,—more than ever nation had before?" Yes, truly, but all that is for the sake of the shop. You would fain sell canvas as well as coals, and crockery as well as iron; you would take every other nation's bread out of its mouth if you could; {3} not being able to do that, your ideal of life is to stand in the thoroughfares of the world, like Ludgate apprentices, screaming to every passer-by, "What d'ye lack?" You know nothing of your own faculties or circumstances; you fancy that, among your damp, flat, fat fields of clay, you can have as quick art-fancy as the Frenchman among his bronzed vines, or the Italian under his volcanic cliffs;—that Art may be learned, as book-keeping is, and when learned, will give you more books to keep. You care for pictures, absolutely, no more than you do for the bills pasted on your dead walls. There is always room on the walls for the bills to be read,—never for the pictures to be seen. You do not know what pictures you have (by repute) in the country, nor whether they are false or true, nor whether they are taken care of or not; in foreign countries, you calmly see the noblest existing pictures in the world rotting in abandoned wreck—(in Venice you saw the Austrian guns deliberately pointed at the palaces containing them), and if you heard that all the fine pictures in Europe were made into sand-bags to-morrow on the Austrian forts, it would not trouble you so much as the chance of a brace or two of game less in your own bags, in a day's shooting. That is your national love of Art.

IV. You have despised Nature; that is to say, all the deep and sacred sensations of natural scenery. The French revolutionists made stables of the cathedrals of France; you have made race-courses of the cathedrals of the earth. Your *one* conception of pleasure is to drive in railroad carriages round their aisles, and eat off their altars.{4} You have put a railroad-bridge over the falls of Schaffhausen. You have tunnelled the cliffs of Lucerne by Tell's chapel; you have destroyed the Clarens shore of the Lake of Geneva; there is not a quiet valley in England that you have not filled with bellowing fire; there is no particle left of English land which you have not trampled coal ashes into {5}—nor any foreign city in which the spread of your presence is not marked among its fair old streets and happy gardens by a consuming white leprosy of new hotels and perfumers' shops: the Alps themselves, which your own poets used to love so reverently, you look upon as soaped poles in a bear-garden, which you set yourselves to climb and slide down again, with "shrieks of delight." When you are past shrieking, having no human articulate voice to say you are glad with, you fill the quietude of their valleys with gunpowder blasts, and rush home, red with cutaneous eruption of conceit, and voluble with convulsive hiccough of self-satisfaction. I think nearly the two sorrowfullest spectacles I have ever seen in humanity, taking the deep inner significance of them, are the English mobs in the valley of Chamouni, amusing themselves with firing rusty howitzers; and the Swiss vintagers of Zurich expressing their Christian thanks for the gift of the vine, by assembling in knots in the "towers of the vineyards," and slowly loading and firing horse-pistols from morning till evening. It is pitiful, to have dim conceptions of duty; more pitiful, it seems to me, to have conceptions like these, of mirth.

Lastly. You despise compassion. There is no need of words of mine for proof of this. ...

§

Measure!—nay, you cannot measure. Who shall measure the difference between the power of those who "do and teach," and who are greatest in the kingdoms of earth, as of heaven—and the power of those who undo, and consume—whose power, at the fullest, is only the power of the moth and the rust? Strange! to think how the Moth-kings lay up treasures for the moth; and the Rust-kings, who are to their peoples' strength as rust to armour, lay up treasures for the rust; and the Robber-kings, treasures for the robber; but how few kings have ever laid up treasures that needed no guarding—treasures of which, the more thieves there were, the better! Broidered robe, only to be rent; helm and sword, only to be dimmed; jewel and gold, only to be scattered;—there have been three kinds of kings who have gathered these. Suppose there ever should arise a Fourth order of kings, who had read, in some obscure writing of long ago, that there was a Fourth kind of treasure, which the jewel and gold could not equal, neither should it be valued with pure gold. A web made fair in the weaving, by Athena's shuttle; an armour, forged in divine fire by Vulcanian force; a gold to be mined in the very sun's red heart, where he sets over the Delphian cliffs;—deep-pictured tissue;—impenetrable armour;—potable gold!—the three great Angels of Conduct, Toil, and Thought, still calling to us, and waiting at the posts of our doors, to lead us, with their winged power, and guide us, with their unerring eyes, by the path which no fowl knoweth, and which the vulture's eye has not seen! Suppose kings should ever arise, who heard and believed this word, and at last gathered and brought forth treasures of — Wisdom — for their people?

Think what an amazing business *that* would be! How inconceivable, in the state of our present national wisdom! That we should bring up our peasants to a book exercise instead of a bayonet exercise!—organise, drill, maintain with pay, and good generalship, armies of thinkers, instead of armies of stabbers!—find national amusement in reading-rooms as well as rifle-grounds; give prizes for a fair shot at a fact, as well as for a leaden splash on a target. What an absurd idea it seems, put fairly in words, that the wealth of the capitalists of civilised nations should ever come to support literature instead of war!

Have yet patience with me, while I read you a single sentence out of the only book, properly to be called a book, that I have yet written myself, the one that will stand (if anything stand), surest and longest of all work of mine.

"It is one very awful form of the operation of wealth in Europe that it is entirely capitalists' wealth which supports unjust wars. Just wars do not need so much money to support them; for most of the men who wage such, wage them gratis; but for an unjust war, men's bodies and souls have both to be bought; and the best tools of war for them besides, which make such war costly to the maximum; not to speak of the cost of base fear, and angry suspicion, between nations which have not grace nor honesty enough in all their multitudes to buy an hour's peace of mind with; as, at present, France and England, purchasing of each other ten millions sterling worth of consternation, annually (a remarkably light crop, half thorns and half aspen leaves, sown, reaped, and granaried by the 'science' of the modern political economist, teaching covetousness instead of truth). And, all unjust war being supportable, if not by pillage of the enemy, only by loans from capitalists, these loans are repaid by subsequent taxation of the people, who appear to have no will in the matter, the capitalists' will being the primary root of the war; but its real root is the covetousness of the whole nation, rendering it incapable of faith, frankness, or justice, and bringing about, therefore, in due time, his own separate loss and punishment to each person."

France and England literally, observe, buy *panic* of each other; they pay, each of them, for ten thousand-thousand-pounds'-worth of terror, a year. Now suppose, instead of buying these ten millions' worth of panic annually, they made up their minds to be at peace with each other, and buy ten millions' worth of knowledge annually; and that each nation spent its ten thousand thousand pounds a year in founding royal libraries, royal art galleries, royal museums, royal gardens, and places of rest. Might it not be better somewhat for both French and English?

It will be long, yet, before that comes to pass. Nevertheless, I hope it will not be long before royal or national libraries will be founded in every considerable city, with a royal series of books in them; the same series in every one of them, chosen books, the best in every kind, prepared for that national series in the most perfect way possible; their text printed all on leaves of equal size, broad of margin, and divided into pleasant volumes, light in the hand, beautiful, and strong, and thorough as examples of binders' work; and that these great libraries will be accessible to all clean and orderly persons at all times of the day and evening; strict law being enforced for this cleanliness and quietness.

I could shape for you other plans, for art-galleries, and for natural history galleries, and for many precious—many, it seems to me, needful—things; but this book plan is the easiest and needfullest, and would prove a considerable tonic to what we call our British constitution, which has fallen dropsical of late, and has an evil thirst, and evil hunger, and wants healthier feeding.

You have got its corn laws repealed for it; try if you cannot get corn laws established for it, dealing in a better bread;—bread made of that old enchanted Arabian grain, the Sesame, which opens doors;—doors not of robbers', but of Kings' Treasuries.

Notes to *Of Kings' Treasuries*

{1}   Since this was written, the answer has become definitely—No; we having surrendered the field of Arctic discovery to the Continental nations, as being ourselves too poor to pay for ships.

{2}   I state this fact without Professor Owen's permission: which of course he could not with propriety have granted, had I asked it; but I consider it so important that the public should be aware of the fact, that I do what seems to me right, though rude.

{3}   That was our real idea of "Free Trade"—"All the trade to myself." You find now that by "competition" other people can manage to sell something as well as you—and now we call for Protection again. Wretches!

{4}   I meant that the beautiful places of the world—Switzerland, Italy, South Germany, and so on—are, indeed, the truest cathedrals—places to be reverent in, and to worship in; and that we only care to drive through them: and to eat and drink at their most sacred places.

{5}   I was singularly struck, some years ago, by finding all the river shore at Richmond, in Yorkshire, black in its earth, from the mere drift of soot-laden air from places many miles away.

5

The Monster Reads!
Mary Shelley Warns About Technology
and the Loss of the Inner Life

by Michael Pastore

But often, in the world's most crowded streets,
But often, in the din of strife,
There rises an unspeakable desire
After the knowledge of our buried life.
— Matthew Arnold

In 1816, the wild poet George Gordon (Lord Byron) challenged his friends, Percy and Mary Shelley, to a contest about writing the best ghost-story. A few evenings later, the three friends discussed the possibility of using galvanism (direct-current electricity produced by chemicals) to bring a corpse back to life. That night, lying in her bed unable to sleep, Mary Shelley conceived the kernel of her novel, *Frankenstein.* About that conception she wrote: "Frightful it must be, for supremely frightful would be the effect of any human endeavour to mock the stupendous mechanism of the creator of the world. His success would terrify the artist; he would rush away from his odious handiwork, horror stricken ... "

Published in England in 1818 when Mary was merely 21, the novel instantly became a smashing success. It is still popular today, although many people mistakenly believe that "Frankenstein" — the surname of the inventor — is the name of the monster.

The story spins around the lives and minds of three main characters. Victor Frankenstein leaves home to study science, then spends two years building an artificial man from spare anatomical parts he has picked up — not on eBay — from butcher shops, dissecting rooms, and vaults that housed dead bodies. Elizabeth Lavenza — kinder than an angel and lovelier than a summer night — waits her entire life to marry Frankenstein, and then experiences the worst wedding night in the history of literature. The monster himself remains unnamed throughout the story, and cannot find one friend or sympathizer in the entire world of not-so-human human beings. The monster's central problem is his low self-esteem caused by his grotesque appearance: tall, dark, and gruesome; awkward in motion; ferocious in strength; cursed with a hideous face that sends everyone who sees it screaming and sprinting for their lives. Alienation increases his frustration. When the monster fails to find human companionship he becomes destructive, perceptively explaining his dysfunction by shouting "I am malicious because I am miserable!"

For a brief span, Frankenstein's creation finds solace, comfort, insight, and wisdom in the imaginary worlds of books. In the middle of the novel, it is books and reading that give the monster courage and self-awareness to reach out to human beings, to reveal his unbearable loneliness, and attempt to change his life. When he secretly observes a family as they read aloud from a work by Volney — *The Ruins, or, Meditation on the Revolutions of Empires and the Law of Nature* — the monster tells how the book "gave me an insight into the manners, governments, and religions of the different nations of the earth." In addition, the reading of *The Ruins* develops his ethical sensibilities: "These wonderful narrations inspired me with strange feelings. Was man, indeed, at once so powerful, so virtuous, so magnificent, yet so vicious and so base? He appeared at one time a mere scion of the evil principle and at another as all that can be conceived as noble and godlike."

The turning point in the novel comes soon after the monster discovers a leather portmanteau filled with three profound books. From Goethe's *Sorrows of Young Werther,* the monster learns about the agonies of thwarted love. In *Lives of the Noble Greeks and Romans,* Plutarch "taught me high thoughts, and elevated me above the wretched sphere of my own reflections, to admire and love the heroes of past ages." Milton's *Paradise Lost* impresses the monster with emotions even deeper. He identifies with Adam and with Satan; feels wretched, helpless, envious and alone; and is "moved with every feeling of wonder and awe."

Leo Tolstoy, Herbert Read, and Erich Fromm are three philosophers who believe that reading, like creativity, makes us more sensitive, empathetic, non-violent and compassionate. What is the cause of the world's widespread violence? .... One cause is the fact that we have not been trained to read great literature, to reflect about books and ideas, and then to develop a humane inner self.

The 20th Century may come to be known as the Age of Extinction, and a provocative book by Barry Sanders (*The Private Death of Public Discourse*) tells us about yet another endangered species: our inner lives. He means what Marcel Proust called "the deep self," the self that is revealed to us whenever we reflect, whenever we engage in a true dialogue with another person, whenever we read books of real significance.

What are the bleak consequences of forgetting our inner space? ... Nothing except escape into unsatisfying substitutes: a conquistadorial zeal for the exploration of outer space; a flighty interest in the paranormal and occult spaces; and an atrophous skydive into cyberspace, the most seductive cyren of them all. Without inner lives, our outer lives become poor, nasty, isolated, brutish, and short on meaningful responses. Anger and meanness pervade our day-to-day existence. Ours is a pent-up aching hostility which too-often erupts into violence: violence in our work, our entertainments, our personal relations, our antagonistic politics.

Sanders's argument begins by examining a number of festering social crises. The bombings of Iraq in 1996. The rising rate of crimes committed by juveniles. The staggering number of Americans in prison or jail, or on parole, or awaiting sentences: 5 million strong. And the 6 million children in America under the age of 6 who live in poverty. What, if anything, can reverse these terrifying trends? Not the shouting and raving on TV-talk shows and the floors of the Congress. Sanders says that the solution is public discourse: talking about these problems in a manner that is calm, intelligent, sincere.

Public discourse is only possible when people possess authentic inner lives. What does this mean, this thing called "inner life"? Inner calm. The slowness of reflective thinking. The richness of a personal imagination. Sanders thinks out loud before us. This inner space, he says, can be nurtured by talking from the heart, and by literacy: by persons capable of reading, "serious and analytical reading, in which people must follow the mazy paths of an argument." He adds: "The passing of literacy also carries to its death analytical thinking and the emotional life."

Our culture has confused the outer and the inner worlds. What happened to talking about — not shouting about — serious issues? The public has become private, and the private has become public. And since nobody is reading anymore, they never the Twain shall meet. As author Neal Gabler points out in *Life The Movie,* our private lives are spectacles, commodities to be sold to talk-show hosts or tabloids. We are dominated by a new and jealous god — Entertainment — which has invaded all aspects of contemporary life: politics, economics, education, business, art, and interpersonal relations.

The result, says Sanders, is "The collapse of a self-sustaining interior life," — which, he claims, may be the most profound change in human development in the whole 20th Century. He writes: "I maintain that interiority began to disappear as reading and writing began to drop out of people's lives, replaced by hours and hours of staring at screens."

"Reading," writes Marcel Proust – in an introduction to a work of Ruskin that hardly mentions either Ruskin or his work — "is that fertile miracle of a communication effected in solitude." Perhaps that is where the problem lies; for Andre Maurois has reminded us that "Men fear silence as they fear solitude, because both give them a glimpse of the terror of life's nothingness." We fear solitude but we need it. For solitude is one necessary condition not only for creative activity, but for the self-reflection that leads to integration and healing of the self.

The most frightening facet of Mary Shelley's novel is this one: that the self-educated monster, who has read three books only, has read more significant literature — and is vastly more self-aware – than the average American male. And thus, *Frankenstein* the book — part science fiction, part horror novel, part gothic romance, and part novel of ideas — remains interesting to this day. It explores questions that still haunt us: Why do children lose their innocence, joyfulness, and goodness when they grow up? Why do men do evil things? How can we distinguish technologies that are dangerous and dehumanizing from the technologies that are beneficent and safe? What are the responsibilities of scientific creators to their inventions, and to these inventions' unintended consequences? and How can we become fully-human human beings, in spite of the knowledge and technologies that drive us from our essential quests?

In portraying Victor Frankenstein as a fallible human — an admixture of wisdom and folly, courage and cowardice, knowledge and ignorance — Mary Shelley has captured our double relationship with knowledge and technology. In his drama *Faust,* Goethe tried to show that the quest for pure knowledge alone is always futile, and often self-destructive. Science can tell us how to make new inventions, yet it never comments about values, about whether or not these inventions are helpful or harmful to humankind. Men who tamper with the bare bones of Technology must always remember what Frankenstein grasped too late. The warm whims of a science that destroys things are at least as prevalent as the scientist's creations that bring us healthier and more comfortable lives.

Prometheus is best known for stealing the gods' fire and giving it to humankind: fire that symbolizes knowledge, science, power, destruction. England had brazenly seized this fire, and the years encompassing the Shelleys' lives were overwhelmed by chaos and uncertainties. The world of 1812 (when Percy Shelley was aged 20 and Mary a teenager of 15) was not so different from own troubled world. War was in full force: in that year the U.S. declared war against Britain; and Napoleon would march an army of 550,000 into Russia then limp back to Paris six months later with merely 20,000 men. In 1812, too, the arts were flourishing. Beethoven completed his 7th and 8th symphonies; Goethe finished his remarkable novel *Wilhelm*

Meister's Apprenticeship; the Grimm brothers first gave us their now-famous fairy tales. And Lord Byron brought "Byronic unhappiness" into our lexicon when he published the first parts of his poem *Childe Harold,* about a man so bored and disgusted with English society that he tries to flee himself by roaming the European world.

What connects us — denizens of the 21st Century — most closely to the era of Mary Shelley is that throughout her lifetime her world was shocked by an unprecedented invasion of technology and rapid change. During the years 1782 to 1812 England was pummeled by scores of inventions that transformed daily life: the steam engine, the oil burner, the threshing machine, the steam-powered rotary motor (which powered cotton-spinning factories), the nail-making machine, the cotton gin, the preserving jar for foods, the first horse-drawn railroad, lithography, electricity from a cell, muskets with interchangeable parts, the submarine, iron trolley tracks, the steamboat, street lighting by gas, the isolation of morphine, rockets introduced as military weapons, and — pardon the pun — the flax machine. And perhaps something that might have better been left undiscovered: techniques for canning food.

The thirty years that followed, 1813 through 1843 (when Mary Shelley was ages 16 to 46) were no less inventive. Here the world acquires the steam locomotive, roads made from crushed stone, the kaleidoscope, the stethoscope, new chemical elements, the flat-bed cylinder press, electromagnetism, thermoelectricity, sound reproduction, iron railroad bridges, waterproof fabric, Portland cement, the galvanometer, Ohm's Law, photography, the typewriter, matches, the telegraph, the reaping machine, the bicycle, rubber, hypnosis, ether for anesthesia, and scientific proof — at last! — that the sperm is essential to fertilization.

The rural life was yielding to the burgeoning urban existence, where the overstressed winners of the rat-race dreamed of building houses in the country hoping to recapture the tranquility of rural life. There were wisps of resistance to this new mechanized culture which threatened to vacuum up the old. In 1811 the Luddites in Northern England began their rebelling by destroying the new machines which whirled their jobs away. But for better or worse, the world of England welcomed this Industrial Revolution which so much determined Shelley's life and literary work.

Mary Shelley — sensitive, perceptive, beautiful soul! — looked into the abyss, and the abyss stared back. She grasped the future and was terrified at what she saw. Mary pre-envisioned the decline of the Romantic spirit: Reason and Science run amok with a god's power without the goddess's compassion. Feeling and Nature would be throttled between the monster's paws. In the desperate loneliness of Frankenstein's monster, we see Mary

Shelley's strength and solitude, and chillingly we feel our own. Love would have healed her; and the true anecdote that follows lets us glimpse the depths of her fearful solitude and her need for love.

In July 1822, 30 days before his 30th birthday, Percy Bysshe Shelley drowned (along with his friend Edward Williams) when the small boat that carried him sank in the Bay of Spezia, off the coast of Italy. His heartbroken friends — Lord Byron, Edward Trelawney, and Leigh Hunt — built a pyre and attempted to burn the corpse. The friends wept as they watched the body disintegrate to ashes. But soon they were astonished to discover that the writer's heart would not burn. For years, the heart was kept by Shelley's friend, Hunt, until at last he was persuaded to return the heart to the devoted widow. For the remainder of her life, Mary kept the withered heart inside the desk where she would write.

Michael Pastore
Ithaca, New York, USA

6
Quotations and Passages About Writing
edited by Michael Pastore

If you wish to be a writer, write.
— Epictetus

The more books we read, the sooner we perceive that the true function of a writer is to produce a masterpiece and that no other task is of any consequence.
— Cyril Connolly

The way to speak and write what shall not go out of fashion is to speak and write sincerely. ... Take Sidney's maxim: "Look into thy heart and write."
— Ralph Waldo Emerson, *Spiritual Laws*

Whenever a sentence came from the true self, and it was felt — it was alive. Be bold, be free, be truthful!
— Brenda Ueland

Art begins when a man wishes to immortalize the most vivid moment he has ever lived.
— Arthur Symons

My method is to take the utmost trouble to find the right thing to say, then say it with the utmost levity.
— George Bernard Shaw

"[Name of toothpaste] has been shown to be an effective decay-preventive dentifrice that can be of significant value when used as directed in a conscientiously applied program of oral hygiene and regular professional care."
— Words of praise, written on boxes of a brand-name toothpaste

Who, with brush or speech, can hope to describe
the divinities of Heaven and Earth?
— Basho Matsuo

People think I can teach them style! What stuff it is. Have something to say and say it is clearly as you can. That is the only secret of style.
— Matthew Arnold

Every man who knows how to read has it in his power to magnify himself, to multiply the ways in which he exists, to make his life full, significant, and interesting.
— Aldous Huxley

The style is the man himself.
— Georges Louis Leclerc de Buffon

The French revolution might be described as a remote but inevitable result of the invention of the art of printing. ... by the aid of books, and of an intercourse with the world of ideas, we are purified, raised, ennobled from savages into intellectual and rational beings.
— William Hazlitt

Our intellectual and active powers increase with our affection. The scholar sits down to write, and all his years of meditation do not furnish him with one good thought or happy expression; but it is necessary to write a letter to a friend, — and, forthwith, troops of gentle thoughts invest themselves, on every hand, with chosen words.
— Ralph Waldo Emerson (from *Friendship*)

There are only three rules for writing a novel. Unfortunately, no one knows what they are.
— Somerset Maugham

Genius is eternal patience.
— Michelangelo

Find a subject you care about and which you in your heart feel others should care about. It is this genuine caring, not your games with language, which will be the most compelling and seductive element in your style.
— Kurt Vonnegut

Always tell the truth in the form of a joke.
— Armenian saying

I should write for the mere yearning and fondness I have for the beautiful, even if my night's labors should be burnt every morning and no eye shine upon them.
— John Keats

If a man could pass through Paradise in a dream, and have a flower presented to him as a pledge that his soul had really been there, and if he found that flower in his hand when he awoke — Ay! and what then?
— Samuel Taylor Coleridge

The storyteller writes because his own experience of men or things has moved him to an emotion so passionate that he can no longer keep it shut up in his heart.
— *The Tale Of The Genji,* 1000 A.D.

Life is terrible and is lived in the streets and in the fields and the place for the writer-to-be, therefore, is in the fields and in the streets. He doesn't explore anything by staying inside, safe from the beetles and the rain. His real subject matter is in the streets and in the courtrooms, in wards, in charity hospital — in all the places where people are in trouble. I think the writer must serve the inarticulate.
— Nelson Algren

Art is not for its own sake,
but as a means of communicating with humanity.
— Modest Mussorgsky

Every scene, even the commonest, is wonderful, if only one can detach oneself, casting off all memory of use and custom, and behold it (as it were) for the first time; in its right, authentic colours; without making comparisons. The novelist should cherish and burnish this faculty of seeing crudely, simply, artlessly, ignorantly; of seeing like a baby or a lunatic, who lives each moment by itself and tarnishes by the present no remembrance of the past.
— Arnold Bennett

The first [way to succeed] is, the stopping off decisively our miscellaneous activity; and concentrating our force on one, or a few points ...
— Ralph Waldo Emerson

There is no more Herculean task than to think a thought about this life and then get it expressed. ... Knowledge does not come to us in details, but in flashes of light from heaven.
— Henry David Thoreau

Paint your Paradise then walk in.
— Nikos Kazantzakis

Write about those things which are sacred and moving and heartbreaking and passionate and joyous to you. Sincerity, sincerity, and more sincerity!
— Michael Pastore

What is it to be admitted to a museum, to see a myriad of particular things, compared with being shown some star's surface, some hard matter in its home! I stand in awe of my body, this matter to which I am bound has become so strange to me. I fear not spirits, ghosts, of which I am one, — *that* my body might, — but I fear bodies, I tremble to meet them. What is this Titan that has possession of me? Talk of mysteries! — Think of our life in nature, — daily to be shown matter, to come in contact with it, — rocks, trees, wind on our cheeks! the *solid* earth! the *actual* world! the *common sense! Contact! Contact! Who* are we? *where* are we?
— Henry David Thoreau

The food of the soul is light and space.
— Herman Melville

I wish I could tell you that in our great land of occasional prosperity, the vital writer can always find an immediate market. But I cannot tell you that. ... The man who has a real ideal of great writing, and has to live by it, will have to tighten up his belt and move into a garret or perhaps into a tent in the wilderness.
— Upton Sinclair

To forget is the same thing as to throw away.
— African saying

Give the mood, and the essay, from the first sentence to the last, grows round it as a cocoon grows round the silkworm.
— Alexander Smith

I see but one rule: to be clear.
— Stendhal

Get down to your real self ... and let that speak. One's real self is always vital and gives the impression of vitality.
– John Burroughs

Do not write about Man, write about one man.
— E. B. White

But James Joyce bores me stiff — too terribly would-be and done-on-purpose, utterly without spontaneity or real life.
— D. H. Lawrence, 1928 (letter to Harry Crosby)

When any extraordinary scene presents itself (as we trust will often be the case), we shall spare no pains nor paper to open it at large to the reader; but if whole years should pass without producing anything worthy of his notice, we shall not be afraid of this and leave such periods of time totally unobserved.
— Henry Fielding

A hunch is creativity trying to tell you something.
— Frank Capra

Every stroke of my brush is the overflow of my inmost heart.
— Sengai

Art is the medium through which men express their deep, real feelings.
— D. H. Lawrence

Neither a lofty degree of intelligence nor imagination nor both together go to the making of genius. Love, love, love that is the soul of genius.
— Wofgang Amadeus Mozart

"Ah!" said a brave painter to me ... "if a man has failed, you will find that he has dreamed instead of working. There is no way to success in our art, but to take off your coat, grind paint, and work like a digger in the railroad, all day and every day."
— Ralph Waldo Emerson

7
The Art of Writing With Sincerity and Style

by Michael Pastore

What is good writing? How does a writer write with sincerity and style?

Advice is plentiful; unfortunately no two writers will agree. Socrates and Democritus would often stand motionless, for days and days, thinking about the answer to one burning question. Schiller, the poet and playwright, could not write without first pulling open a desk drawer, then smelling a lump of rotten apples, which reminded him of his childhood home. Hemingway wrote standing up. Voltaire wrote lying down, using the naked back of his mistress as a desk.

Though all writers disagree on techniques or habits, many writers recommend some simple principles for guiding their own writing, and for teaching writing students to express themselves with clarity and power. In addition to "Practice, practice, practice!", three suggestions are:

1. Writers learn to write by reading great books.
2. Writers write best about the subjects they care deeply about.
3. Writers imagine one ideal reader when they write.

This last line of good advice was first suggested by the American philosopher Ralph Waldo Emerson, in an essay *Friendship:*

"Our intellectual and active powers increase with our affection. The scholar sits down to write, and all his years of meditation do not furnish him with one good thought or happy expression; but it is necessary to write a letter to a friend — and, forthwith, troops of gentle thoughts invest themselves, on every hand, with chosen words."

Creative persons in many fields — artists, scientists, mathematicians, inventors, and writers — frequently use some variety of a six-step creative process. Writers who grasp the process can write about any subject, and in every genre. Writers who use this method discover that "writer's block" melts like a cube of ice.

The six parts of this creative writing process are:

A. Gather Original Ideas
B. Play With These Ideas (Explore, deepen, invent, connect)
C. Work With The Ideas (Choose genre and audience; make outlines)
D. Incubate (Relax and let the unconscious mind work on the ideas)
E. Write From the Heart (Write quickly, without stopping)
F. Rest, then Rewrite

About one hundred years ago, literary theory favored a slow and crafted approach to writing, where stories and poems were composed ever-so-cautiously, like building a mansion by laying bricks. Hours and even days might be consumed in searching for the one and only perfect sentence or word. Oscar Wilde satirized this over-emphasis on refinement, when he quipped: "I spent the whole morning putting in a comma — and the whole afternoon taking it out again."

Modern theory favors a much less restrained approach to writing. Writers today seek to tap the vast resources of the unconscious. "Write hot, rewrite cool," is the working motto. The attempt to get everything down, as quickly as possible, by writing without stopping, has been summarized neatly by Jacques Barzun:

" ... the heat of writing. I call it heat not because one does or should write in a fever, but because the deliberate choice of words and links and transitions is easiest and best when it is made from a throng of ideas bubbling under the surface of consciousness. On this account, I strongly recommend writing ahead full tilt, not stopping to correct. Cross out no more than a few words that will permit you to go on when you foresee a blind alley. Leave some words in a blank, some sentences not complete. Keep going!"

The goal of it all, of course, is good writing. Good writing is clear, interesting, and truthful. A simple and savvy definition epitomizes these qualities: "Good writing is original, and the way to be original is to be sincere." Listen again to Mr. Emerson, in his essay: *Goethe, or, The Writer*, as he explains how the style and the man are one:

"It makes a great difference to the force of any sentence, whether there be a man behind it, or no. In the learned journal, in the influential newspaper, I discern no form; only some irresponsible shadow; oftener some monied corporation, or some dangler, who hopes, in the mask and robes of his paragraph, to pass for somebody. But, through every clause and part of speech of a right book, I meet the eyes of the most determined of men: his force and terror inundate every word: the commas and dashes are alive; so that the writing is athletic and nimble, — can go far and live long."

Once again we return to the essential question: How can we learn to write well? ... The great goal of every writer is to find her Voice. Bertrand Russell began by imitating the masters, then discovered himself at last.

"A style is not good unless it is an intimate and almost involuntary expression of the personality of the writer, and then only if the writer's personality is worth expressing. But although direct imitation is always to be deprecated, there is much to be gained by familiarity with good prose, especially in cultivating a sense for prose rhythm."

When a writer finds her Voice she writes naturally and freely, drawing energy and wisdom from the deepest and sincerest place within. Meaning melds with style the same way form fits function. The writer achieves mastery of her art and craft; the writing becomes a force of Nature, touching the reader with simplicity and power. "Nature is perfect," wrote Leonardo da Vinci, "because in the works of Nature nothing is lacking and nothing is superfluous."

Style, in great writing, is the sincerest expression of the author's inmost self. Great style is clear, concise, and captivating — nothing is lacking, nothing is superfluous. Whenever we read great writing something genuine in it moves us, in waves of resonance and recognition, with rays of wonder and delight.

8
Secrets of the Great Writers

by Anatole France

All great authors write badly. That is well known. At least, the pedants say so. Great writers are impetuous. The vigour of their vocabulary, the intensity of their style, the daring of their phrases, disconcert the pedants. To the pundits good writing apparently means writing according to rules. But born writers make their own rules, or rather make none. They change their manner at every moment, as inspiration dictates, sometimes they are harmonious, sometimes rugged, sometimes indolent and sometimes spirited. So, according to the common notion, they cannot write well. And why deny it? Rabelais is not free from faults. Hit litanies of nouns, his string of epithets, his lines of verbs, undoubtedly prove his inexhaustible imagination, but they make his style heavy. His phrases often lack suppleness, cadence and balance. ... The "Contes" of the Seigneur des Accords are full of charm. His style flows and is a delight to the ear. It is better than that of Rabelais. Nevertheless, it is Rabelais who is the great writer, and not the Seigneur des Accords.

Yes, indeed, Moliere also writes badly, and so do Saint-Simon, and Balzac, and all the others, I tell you! In Moliere's time, certain writers, Saint-Evremond and Furetiere, for example, used a much more polished syntax. They were purer. Only, Moliere is Moliere, that is to say, not a good, but a great writer.

§

Great authors have eternal qualities. If the slightest trifle from their pen enchants us, it is because a wise head and a sensitive heart always guide their hand.

It is a matter of indifference that their syntax is a little shaky, since these very slips are evidence of the powerful drive of the mind which is guilty of the atrocities. It is the syntax of passion.

It is a matter of indifference that they pillage right and left, and that sometimes they get mixed up in the plot of their stories. What matters in them is, not the story, however beautifully told, but the opinions and ideas which it clothes. Like nurses rocking babies, they spin us, haphazardly, adorable stories which go back to the beginning of time. We eagerly swallow the bait, and there is wisdom concealed in the honey of their fables. Thus, in the course of centuries, the same anecdotes serve to express the varying thoughts of the most enlightened men.

All really great men have the prime virtue of sincerity. They extirpate hypocrisy from their hearts; they bravely reveal their weaknesses, their doubts, their vices. They dissect themselves. They expose their bared souls, so that all their contemporaries may recognize themselves in this picture, and reject the lies which corrupt their lives. They are courageous. They are not afraid to challenge prejudices. No power, civil, moral or immoral, can impose upon them.

Sometimes, it is true, frankness is so dangerous that it would cost them their liberty or even their lives. Under the most liberal, as under the most tyrannical governments, to proclaim what will be recognized as just and right fifty or a hundred years later is sufficient to incur imprisonment or the scaffold.

As it is better to speak than to be silent, the wise often behave like fools, in order not to be gagged. They gambol, shake their cap and bells, and give utterance to the most reasonable follies. They are allowed to caper because they are taken for buffoons. This stratagem must not be held against them. Concerning the opinions which he held dearly, Rabelais used to say mockingly: "I will maintain them to the stake ... exclusively." Was he wrong? And if he had gone to the stake, would it now be possible for us to enjoy his pantagruelism?

Great writers have not mean souls. That, Mr. Brown, is all their secret.

They profoundly love their fellow-men. They are generous — they do not limit their affections. They pity all suffering, and strive to soothe it. They take compassion on the poor players who perform in the comic tragedy, or the tragi-comedy, of destiny. Pity, you see, is the very basis of genius, Professor.

9
Writing Novels

by Arnold Bennett

I

The novelist is he who, having seen life, and being so excited by it that he absolutely must transmit the vision to others, chooses narrative fiction as the liveliest vehicle for the relief of his feelings. He is like other artists — he cannot remain silent; he cannot keep himself to himself, he is bursting with the news; he is bound to tell — the affair is too thrilling! Only he differs from most artists in this — that what most chiefly strikes him is the indefinable humanness of human nature, the large general manner of existing. Of course, he is the result of evolution from the primitive. And you can see primitive novelists to this day transmitting to acquaintances their fragmentary and crude visions of life in the café or the club, or on the kerbstone. They belong to the lowest circle of artists; but they are artists; and the form that they adopt is the very basis of the novel. By innumerable entertaining steps from them you may ascend to the major artist whose vision of life, inclusive, intricate and intense, requires for its due transmission the great traditional form of the novel as perfected by the masters of a long age which has temporarily set the novel higher than any other art-form.

I would not argue that the novel should be counted supreme among the great traditional forms of art. Even if there is a greatest form, I do not much care which it is. I have in turn been convinced that Chartres Cathedral, certain Greek sculpture, Mozart's *Don Juan*, and the juggling of Paul Cinquevalli, was the finest thing in the world — not to mention the achievements of Shakspere or Nijinsky. But there is something to be said for the real pre-eminence of prose fiction as a literary form. (Even the modern epic has learnt almost all it knows from prose-fiction.) The novel has, and always will have, the advantage of its comprehensive bigness. St Peter's at Rome is a trifle compared with Tolstoi's *War and Peace;* and it is as certain as anything can be that, during the present geological epoch at any rate, no epic half as long as *War and Peace* will ever be read, even if written.

Notoriously the novelist (including the playwright, who is a sub-novelist) has been taking the bread out of the mouths of other artists. In the matter of poaching, the painter has done a lot, and the composer has done more, but what the painter and the composer have done is as naught compared to the grasping deeds of the novelist. And whereas the painter and the composer have got into difficulties with their audacious schemes, the novelist has poached, colonised, and annexed with a success that is not denied. There is scarcely any aspect of the interestingness of life which is not now rendered in prose fiction — from landscape-painting to sociology — and none which might not be. Unnecessary to go back to the ante-Scott age in order to perceive how the novel has aggrandised itself! It has conquered enormous territories even since *Germinal*. Within the last fifteen years it has gained. Were it to adopt the hue of the British Empire, the entire map of the universe would soon be coloured red. Wherever it ought to stand in the hierarchy of forms, it has, actually, no rival at the present day as a means for transmitting the impassioned vision of life. It is, and will be for some time to come, the form to which the artist with the most inclusive vision instinctively turns, because it is the most inclusive form, and the most adaptable. Indeed, before we are much older, if its present rate of progress continues, it will have reoccupied the dazzling position to which the mighty Balzac lifted it, and in which he left it in 1850. So much, by the way, for the rank of the novel.

II

In considering the equipment of the novelist there are two attributes which may always be taken for granted. The first is the sense of beauty — indispensable to the creative artist. Every creative artist has it, in his degree. He is an artist because he has it. An artist works under the stress of instinct. No man's instinct can draw him towards material which repels him — the fact is obvious. Obviously, whatever kind of life the novelist writes about, he has been charmed and seduced by it, he is under its spell — that is, he has seen beauty in it. He could have no other reason for writing about it. He may see a strange sort of beauty; he may — indeed he does — see a sort of beauty that nobody has quite seen before; he may see a sort of beauty that none save a few odd spirits ever will or can be made to see. But he does see beauty. To say, after reading a novel which has held you, that the author has no sense of beauty, is inept. (The mere fact that you turned over his pages with interest is an answer to the criticism — a criticism, indeed, which is not more sagacious than that of the reviewer who remarks: "Mr Blank has produced a thrilling novel, but unfortunately he cannot write." Mr Blank has written; and he could, anyhow, write enough to thrill the reviewer.) All that a wise person will assert is that an artist's sense of beauty is different for the time being from his own.

The reproach of the lack of a sense of beauty has been brought against nearly all original novelists; it is seldom brought against a mediocre novelist. Even in the extreme cases it is untrue; perhaps it is most untrue in the extreme cases. I do not mean such a case as that of Zola, who never went to extremes. I mean, for example, Gissing, a real extremist, who, it is now admitted, saw a clear and undiscovered beauty in forms of existence which hitherto no artist had deigned seriously to examine. And I mean Huysmans, a case even more extreme. Possibly no works have been more abused for ugliness than Huysman's novel *En Ménage* and his book of descriptive essays *De Tout*. Both reproduce with exasperation what is generally regarded as the sordid ugliness of commonplace daily life. Yet both exercise a unique charm (and will surely be read when *La Cathédrale* is forgotten). And it is inconceivable that Huysmans — whatever he may have said — was not ravished by the secret beauty of his subjects and did not exult in it.

The other attribute which may be taken for granted in the novelist, as in every artist, is passionate intensity of vision. Unless the vision is passionately intense the artist will not be moved to transmit it. He will not be inconvenienced by it; and the motive to pass it on will thus not exist. Every fine emotion produced in the reader has been, and must have been, previously felt by the writer, but in a far greater degree. It is not altogether uncommon to hear a reader whose heart has been desolated by the poignancy of a narrative complain that the writer is unemotional. Such people have no notion at all of the processes of artistic creation.

III

A sense of beauty and a passionate intensity of vision being taken for granted, the one other important attribute in the equipment of the novelist — the attribute which indeed by itself practically suffices, and whose absence renders futile all the rest — is fineness of mind. A great novelist must have great qualities of mind. His mind must be sympathetic, quickly responsive, courageous, honest, humorous, tender, just, merciful. He must be able to conceive the ideal without losing sight of the fact that it is a human world we live in. Above all, his mind must be permeated and controlled by common sense. His mind, in a word, must have the quality of being noble. Unless his mind is all this, he will never, at the ultimate bar, be reckoned supreme. That which counts, on every page, and all the time, is the very texture of his mind — the glass through which he sees things. Every other attribute is secondary, and is dispensable. Fielding lives unequalled among English novelists because the broad nobility of his mind is unequalled. He is read with unreserved enthusiasm because the reader feels himself at each paragraph to be in close contact with a glorious personality. And no advance in technique among later novelists can possibly imperil his position. He will take second place when a more noble mind, a more superb common sense, happens to wield the narrative pen, and not before. What undermines the renown of Dickens is the growing conviction that the texture of his mind was common, that he fell short in courageous facing of the truth, and in certain delicacies of perception. As much may be said of Thackeray, whose mind was somewhat incomplete for so grandiose a figure, and not free from defects which are inimical to immortality.

It is a hard saying for me, and full of danger in any country whose artists have shown contempt for form, yet I am obliged to say that, as the years pass, I attach less and less importance to good technique in fiction. I love it, and I have fought for a better recognition of its importance in England, but I now have to admit that the modern history of fiction will not support me. With the single exception of Turgenev, the great novelists of the world, according to my own standards, have either ignored technique or have failed to understand it. What an error to suppose that the finest foreign novels show a better sense of form than the finest English novels! Balzac was a prodigious blunderer. He could not even manage a sentence, not to speak of the general form of a book. And as for a greater than Balzac — Stendhal — his scorn of technique was notorious. Stendhal was capable of writing, in a masterpiece: "By the way I ought to have told you earlier that the Duchess — !" And as for a greater than either Balzac or Stendhal — Dostoievsky — what a hasty, amorphous lump of gold is the sublime, the unapproachable Brothers Karamazov! Any tutor in a college for teaching the whole art of fiction by post in twelve lessons could show where Dostoievsky was clumsy and careless. What would have been Flaubert's detailed criticism of that book? And what would it matter? And, to take a minor example, witness the comically amateurish technique of the late "Mark Rutherford"— nevertheless a novelist whom one can deeply admire.

And when we come to consider the great technicians, Guy de Maupassant and Flaubert, can we say that their technique will save them, or atone in the slightest degree for the defects of their minds? Exceptional artists both, they are both now inevitably falling in esteem to the level of the second-rate. Human nature being what it is, and de Maupassant being tinged with eroticism, his work is sure to be read with interest by mankind; but he is already classed. Nobody, now, despite all his brilliant excellences, would dream of putting de Maupassant with the first magnitudes. And the declension of Flaubert is one of the outstanding phenomena of modern French criticism. It is being discovered that Flaubert's mind was not quite noble enough — that, indeed, it was a cruel mind, and a little anaemic.

Bouvard et Pécuchet was the crowning proof that Flaubert had lost sight of the humanness of the world, and suffered from the delusion that he had been born on the wrong planet. The glitter of his technique is dulled now, and fools even count it against him. In regard to one section of human activity only did his mind seem noble — namely, literary technique. His correspondence, written, of course, currently, was largely occupied with the question of literary technique, and his correspondence stands forth to-day as his best work — a marvellous fount of inspiration to his fellow artists. So I return to the point that the novelist's one important attribute (beyond the two postulated) is fundamental quality of mind. It and nothing else makes both the friends and the enemies which he has; while the influence of technique is slight and transitory. And I repeat that it is a hard saying.

I begin to think that great writers of fiction are by the mysterious nature of their art ordained to be "amateurs." There may be something of the amateur in all great artists. I do not know why it should be so, unless because, in the exuberance of their sense of power, they are impatient of the exactitudes of systematic study and the mere bother of repeated attempts to arrive at a minor perfection. Assuredly no great artist was ever a profound scholar. The great artist has other ends to achieve. And every artist, major and minor, is aware in his conscience that art is full of artifice, and that the desire to proceed rapidly with the affair of creation, and an excusable dislike of re-creating anything twice, thrice, or ten times over — unnatural task! — are responsible for much of that artifice. We can all point in excuse to Shakspere, who was a very rough-and-ready person, and whose methods would shock Flaubert. Indeed, the amateurishness of Shakspere has been mightily exposed of late years. But nobody seems to care. If Flaubert had been a greater artist he might have been more of an amateur.

IV

Of this poor neglected matter of technique the more important branch is design — or construction. It is the branch of the art — of all arts — which comes next after "inspiration" — a capacious word meant to include everything that the artist must be born with and cannot acquire. The less important branch of technique — far less important — may be described as an ornamentation.

There are very few rules of design in the novel; but the few are capital. Nevertheless, great novelists have often flouted or ignored them — to the detriment of their work. In my opinion the first rule is that the interest must be centralised; it must not be diffused equally over various parts of the canvas. To compare one art with another may be perilous, but really the convenience of describing a novel as a canvas is extreme. In a well-designed picture the eye is drawn chiefly to one particular spot. If the eye is drawn with equal force to several different spots, then we reproach the painter for having "scattered" the interest of the picture. Similarly with the novel. A novel must have one, two, or three figures that easily overtop the rest. These figures must be in the foreground, and the rest in the middle-distance or in the back-ground.

Moreover, these figures — whether they are saints or sinners — must somehow be presented more sympathetically than the others. If this cannot be done, then the inspiration is at fault. The single motive that should govern the choice of a principal figure is the motive of love for that figure. What else could the motive be? The race of heroes is essential to art. But what makes a hero is less the deeds of the figure chosen than the understanding sympathy of the artist with the figure. To say that the hero has disappeared from modern fiction is absurd. All that has happened is that the characteristics of the hero have changed, naturally, with the times. When Thackeray wrote "a novel without a hero," he wrote a novel with a first-class hero, and nobody knew this better than Thackeray. What he meant was that he was sick of the conventional bundle of characteristics styled a hero in his day, and that he had changed the type. Since then we have grown sick of Dobbins, and the type has been changed again more than once. The fateful hour will arrive when we shall be sick of Ponderevos.

The temptation of the great novelist, overflowing with creative force, is to scatter the interest. In both his major works Tolstoi found the temptation too strong for him. *Anna Karenina* is not one novel, but two, and suffers accordingly. As for *War and Peace,* the reader wanders about in it as in a forest, for days, lost, deprived of a sense of direction, and with no vestige of a sign-post; at intervals encountering mysterious faces whose identity he in vain tries to recall. On a much smaller scale Meredith committed the same error. Who could assert positively which of the sisters Fleming is the heroine of *Rhoda Fleming* ? For nearly two hundred pages at a stretch Rhoda scarcely appears. And more than once the author seems quite to forget that the little knave Algernon is not, after all, the hero of the story.

The second rule of design — perhaps in the main merely a different view of the first — is that the interest must be maintained. It may increase, but it must never diminish. Here is that special aspect of design which we call construction, or plot. By interest I mean the interest of the story itself, and not the interest of the continual play of the author's mind on his material. In proportion as the interest of the story is maintained, the plot is a good one. In so far as it lapses, the plot is a bad one. There is no other criterion of good construction. Readers of a certain class are apt to call good the plot of that story in which "you can't tell what is going to happen next." But in some of the most tedious novels ever written you can't tell what is going to happen next — and you don't care a fig what is going to happen next. It would be nearer the mark to say that the plot is good when "you want to make sure what will happen next"! Good plots set you anxiously guessing what will happen next.

When the reader is misled—not intentionally in order to get an effect, but clumsily through amateurishness — then the construction is bad. This calamity does not often occur in fine novels, but in really good work another calamity does occur with far too much frequency — namely, the tantalising of the reader at a critical point by a purposeless, wanton, or negligent shifting of the interest from the major to the minor theme. A sad example of this infantile trick is to be found in the thirty-first chapter of *Rhoda Fleming,* wherein, well knowing that the reader is tingling for the interview between Roberts and Rhoda, the author, unable to control his own capricious and monstrous fancy for Algernon, devotes some sixteen pages to the young knave's vagaries with an illicit thousand pounds. That the sixteen pages are excessively brilliant does not a bit excuse the wilful unshapeliness of the book's design.

The Edwardian and Georgian out-and-out defenders of Victorian fiction are wont to argue that though the event-plot in sundry great novels may be loose and casual (that is to say, simply careless), the "idea-plot" is usually close-knit, coherent, and logical. I have never yet been able to comprehend how an idea-plot can exist independently of an event-plot (any more than how spirit can be conceived apart from matter); but assuming that an idea-plot can exist independently, and that the mysterious thing is superior in form to its coarse fellow, the event-plot (which I positively do not believe), — even then I still hold that sloppiness in the fabrication of the event-plot amounts to a grave iniquity. In this connection I have in mind, among English novels, chiefly the work of "Mark Rutherford,"{1} George Eliot, the Brontës, and Anthony Trollope.

The one other important rule in construction is that the plot should be kept throughout within the same convention. All plots — even those of our most sacred naturalistic contemporaries — are and must be a conventionalisation of life. We imagine we have arrived at a convention which is nearer to the truth of life than that of our forerunners. Perhaps we have — but so little nearer that the difference is scarcely appreciable! An aviator at midday may be nearer the sun than the motorist, but regarded as a portion of the entire journey to the sun, the aviator's progress upward can safely be ignored. No novelist has yet, or ever will, come within a hundred million miles of life itself. It is impossible for us to see how far we still are from life. The defects of a new convention disclose themselves late in its career. The notion that "naturalists" have at last lighted on a final formula which ensures truth to life is ridiculous. "Naturalist" is merely an epithet expressing self-satisfaction.

Similarly, the habit of deriding as "conventional" plots constructed in an earlier convention, is ridiculous. Under this head Dickens in particular has been assaulted; I have assaulted him myself. But within their convention, the plots of Dickens are excellent, and show little trace of amateurishness, and every sign of skilled accomplishment. And Dickens did not blunder out of one convention into another, as certain of ourselves undeniably do. Thomas Hardy, too, has been arraigned for the conventionalism of his plots. And yet Hardy happens to be one of the rare novelists who have evolved a new convention to suit their idiosyncrasy. Hardy's idiosyncrasy is a deep conviction of the whimsicality of the divine power, and again and again he has expressed this with a virtuosity of skill which ought to have put humility into the hearts of naturalists, but which has not done so. The plot of *The Woodlanders* is one of the most exquisite examples of subtle symbolic illustration of an idea that a writer of fiction ever achieved; it makes the symbolism of Ibsen seem crude. You may say that *The Woodlanders* could not have occurred in real life. No novel could have occurred in real life. The balance of probabilities is incalculably against any novel whatsoever; and rightly so. A convention is essential, and the duty of a novelist is to be true within his chosen convention, and not further. Most novelists still fail in this duty. Is there any reason, indeed, why we should be so vastly cleverer than our fathers? I do not think we are.

V

Leaving the seductive minor question of ornamentation, I come lastly to the question of getting the semblance of life on to the page before the eyes of the reader — the daily and hourly texture of existence. The novelist has selected his subject; he has drenched himself in his subject. He has laid down the main features of the design. The living embryo is there, and waits to be developed into full organic structure. Whence and how does the novelist obtain the vital tissue which must be his material? The answer is that he digs it out of himself. First-class fiction is, and must be, in the final resort autobiographical. What else should it be? The novelist may take notes of phenomena likely to be of use to him. And he may acquire the skill to invent very apposite illustrative incident. But he cannot invent psychology. Upon occasion some human being may entrust him with confidences extremely precious for his craft. But such windfalls are so rare as to be negligible. From outward symptoms he can guess something of the psychology of others. He can use a real person as the unrecognisable but helpful basis for each of his characters.... And all that is nothing. And all special research is nothing. When the real intimate work of creation has to be done — and it has to be done on every page — the novelist can only look within for effective aid. Almost solely by arranging and modifying what he has felt and seen, and scarcely at all by inventing, can he accomplish his end. An inquiry into the career of any first-class novelist invariably reveals that his novels are full of autobiography. But, as a fact, every good novel contains far more autobiography than any inquiry could reveal. Episodes, moods, characters of autobiography can be detected and traced to their origin by critical acumen, but the intimate autobiography that runs through each page, vitalising it, may not be detected. In dealing with each character in each episode the novelist must for a thousand convincing details interrogate that part of his own individuality which corresponds to the particular character. The foundation of his equipment is universal sympathy. And the result of this (or the cause — I don't know which) is that in his own individuality there is something of everybody. If he is a born novelist he is safe in asking himself, when in doubt as to the behaviour of a given personage at a given point: "Now, what should *I* have done?" And incorporating the answer! And this in practice is what he does. Good fiction is autobiography dressed in the colours of all mankind.

The necessarily autobiographical nature of fiction accounts for the creative repetition to which all novelists — including the most powerful — are reduced. They monotonously yield again and again to the strongest predilections of their own individuality. Again and again they think they are creating, by observation, a quite new character — and lo! when finished it is an old one — autobiographical psychology has triumphed! A novelist may achieve a reputation with only a single type, created and re-created in varying forms. And the very greatest do not contrive to create more than half a score genuine separate types. In Cerfberr and Christophe's biographical dictionary of the characters of Balzac, a tall volume of six hundred pages, there are some two thousand entries of different individuals, but probably fewer than a dozen genuine distinctive types. No creative artist ever repeated himself more brazenly or more successfully than Balzac. His miser, his vicious delightful actress, his vicious delightful duchess, his young man-about-town, his virtuous young man, his heroic weeping virgin, his angelic wife and mother, his poor relation, and his faithful stupid servant — each is continually popping up with a new name in the *Human Comedy.* A similar phenomenon, as Frank Harris has proved, is to be observed in Shakspere. Hamlet of Denmark was only the last and greatest of a series of Shaksperean Hamlets.

It may be asked, finally: What of the actual process of handling the raw material dug out of existence and of the artist's self — the process of transmuting life into art? There is no process. That is to say, there is no conscious process. The convention chosen by an artist is his illusion of the truth. Consciously, the artist only omits, selects, arranges. But let him beware of being false to his illusion, for then the process becomes conscious, and bad. This is sentimentality, which is the seed of death in his work. Every artist is tempted to sentimentalise, or to be cynical — practically the same thing. And when he falls to the temptation, the reader whispers in his heart, be it only for one instant: "That is not true to life." And in turn the reader's illusion of reality is impaired. Readers are divided into two classes — the enemies and the friends of the artist. The former, a legion, admire for a fortnight or a year. They hate an uncompromising struggle for the truth. They positively like the artist to fall to temptation. If he falls, they exclaim, "How sweet!" The latter are capable of savouring the fine unpleasantness of the struggle for truth. And when they whisper in their hearts: "That is not true to life," they are ashamed for the artist. They are few, very few; but a vigorous clan. It is they who confer immortality.

{1} Mark Rutherford is the pseudonym of the author William Hale White (1831–1913). His book *Mark Rutherford's Deliverance* (1885) was called by George Orwell, "The best novel written in English." (MP)

10
Modern Fiction

by Virginia Woolf

In making any survey, even the freest and loosest, of modern fiction, it is difficult not to take it for granted that the modern practice of the art is somehow an improvement upon the old. With their simple tools and primitive materials, it might be said, Fielding did well and Jane Austen even better, but compare their opportunities with ours! Their masterpieces certainly have a strange air of simplicity. And yet the analogy between literature and the process, to choose an example, of making motor cars scarcely holds good beyond the first glance. It is doubtful whether in the course of the centuries, though we have learnt much about making machines, we have learnt anything about making literature. We do not come to write better; all that we can be said to do is to keep moving, now a little in this direction, now in that, but with a circular tendency should the whole course of the track be viewed from a sufficiently lofty pinnacle. It need scarcely be said that we make no claim to stand, even momentarily, upon that vantage ground. On the flat, in the crowd, half blind with dust, we look back with envy to those happier warriors, whose battle is won and whose achievements wear so serene an air of accomplishment that we can scarcely refrain from whispering that the fight was not so fierce for them as for us. It is for the historian of literature to decide; for him to say if we are now beginning or ending or standing in the middle of a great period of prose fiction, for down in the plain little is visible. We only know that certain gratitudes and hostilities inspire us; that certain paths seem to lead to fertile land, others to the dust and the desert; and of this perhaps it may be worth while to attempt some account.

Our quarrel, then, is not with the classics, and if we speak of quarrelling with Mr. Wells, Mr. Bennett, and Mr. Galsworthy, it is partly that by the mere fact of their existence in the flesh their work has a living, breathing, everyday imperfection which bids us take what liberties with it we choose. But it is also true that, while we thank them for a thousand gifts, we reserve our unconditional gratitude for Mr. Hardy, for Mr. Conrad, and in a much lesser degree for the Mr. Hudson of *The Purple Land, Green Mansions,*

and *Far Away and Long Ago.* Mr. Wells, Mr. Bennett, and Mr. Galsworthy
have excited so many hopes and disappointed them so persistently that our
gratitude largely takes the form of thanking them for having shown us what
they might have done but have not done; what we certainly could not do,
but as certainly, perhaps, do not wish to do. No single phrase will sum up
the charge or grievance which we have to bring against a mass of work so
large in its volume and embodying so many qualities, both admirable and
the reverse. If we tried to formulate our meaning in one word we should
say that these three writers are materialists. It is because they are concerned
not with the spirit but with the body that they have disappointed us, and left
us with the feeling that the sooner English fiction turns its back upon them,
as politely as may be, and marches, if only into the desert, the better for its
soul. Naturally, no single word reaches the centre of three separate targets.
In the case of Mr. Wells it falls notably wide of the mark. And yet even
with him it indicates to our thinking the fatal alloy in his genius, the great
clod of clay that has got itself mixed up with the purity of his inspiration.
But Mr. Bennett is perhaps the worst culprit of the three, inasmuch as he
is by far the best workman. He can make a book so well constructed and
solid in its craftsmanship that it is difficult for the most exacting of critics
to see through what chink or crevice decay can creep in. There is not so
much as a draught between the frames of the windows, or a crack in the
boards. And yet — if life should refuse to live there? That is a risk which
the creator of *The Old Wives' Tale,* George Cannon, Edwin Clayhanger, and
hosts of other figures, may well claim to have surmounted. His characters
live abundantly, even unexpectedly, but it remains to ask how do they live,
and what do they live for? More and more they seem to us, deserting even
the well-built villa in the Five Towns, to spend their time in some softly
padded first-class railway carriage, pressing bells and buttons innumerable;
and the destiny to which they travel so luxuriously becomes more and
more unquestionably an eternity of bliss spent in the very best hotel in
Brighton. It can scarcely be said of Mr. Wells that he is a materialist in
the sense that he takes too much delight in the solidity of his fabric. His
mind is too generous in its sympathies to allow him to spend much time
in making things shipshape and substantial. He is a materialist from sheer
goodness of heart, taking upon his shoulders the work that ought to have
been discharged by Government officials, and in the plethora of his ideas
and facts scarcely having leisure to realise, or forgetting to think important,
the crudity and coarseness of his human beings. Yet what more damaging
criticism can there be both of his earth and of his Heaven than that they are
to be inhabited here and hereafter by his Joans and his Peters? Does not
the inferiority of their natures tarnish whatever institutions and ideals may
be provided for them by the generosity of their creator? Nor, profoundly

though we respect the integrity and humanity of Mr. Galsworthy, shall we find what we seek in his pages.

If we fasten, then, one label on all these books, on which is one word materialists, we mean by it that they write of unimportant things; that they spend immense skill and immense industry making the trivial and the transitory appear the true and the enduring.

We have to admit that we are exacting, and, further, that we find it difficult to justify our discontent by explaining what it is that we exact. We frame our question differently at different times. But it reappears most persistently as we drop the finished novel on the crest of a sigh — Is it worth while? What is the point of it all? Can it be that, owing to one of those little deviations which the human spirit seems to make from time to time, Mr. Bennett has come down with his magnificent apparatus for catching life just an inch or two on the wrong side? Life escapes; and perhaps without life nothing else is worth while. It is a confession of vagueness to have to make use of such a figure as this, but we scarcely better the matter by speaking, as critics are prone to do, of reality. Admitting the vagueness which afflicts all criticism of novels, let us hazard the opinion that for us at this moment the form of fiction most in vogue more often misses than secures the thing we seek. Whether we call it life or spirit, truth or reality, this, the essential thing, has moved off, or on, and refuses to be contained any longer in such ill-fitting vestments as we provide. Nevertheless, we go on perseveringly, conscientiously, constructing our two and thirty chapters after a design which more and more ceases to resemble the vision in our minds. So much of the enormous labour of proving the solidity, the likeness to life, of the story is not merely labour thrown away but labour misplaced to the extent of obscuring and blotting out the light of the conception. The writer seems constrained, not by his own free will but by some powerful and unscrupulous tyrant who has him in thrall, to provide a plot, to provide comedy, tragedy, love interest, and an air of probability embalming the whole so impeccable that if all his figures were to come to life they would find themselves dressed down to the last button of their coats in the fashion of the hour. The tyrant is obeyed; the novel is done to a turn. But sometimes, more and more often as time goes by, we suspect a momentary doubt, a spasm of rebellion, as the pages fill themselves in the customary way. Is life like this? Must novels be like this?

Look within and life, it seems, is very far from being "like this". Examine for a moment an ordinary mind on an ordinary day. The mind receives a myriad impressions—trivial, fantastic, evanescent, or engraved with the sharpness of steel. From all sides they come, an incessant shower of innumerable atoms; and as they fall, as they shape themselves into the life of Monday or Tuesday, the accent falls differently from of old; the moment of importance came not here but there; so that, if a writer were a free man and not a slave, if he could write what he chose, not what he must, if he could base his work upon his own feeling and not upon convention, there would be no plot, no comedy, no tragedy, no love interest or catastrophe in the accepted style, and perhaps not a single button sewn on as the Bond Street tailors would have it. Life is not a series of gig lamps symmetrically arranged; life is a luminous halo, a semi-transparent envelope surrounding us from the beginning of consciousness to the end. Is it not the task of the novelist to convey this varying, this unknown and uncircumscribed spirit, whatever aberration or complexity it may display, with as little mixture of the alien and external as possible? We are not pleading merely for courage and sincerity; we are suggesting that the proper stuff of fiction is a little other than custom would have us believe it.

It is, at any rate, in some such fashion as this that we seek to define the quality which distinguishes the work of several young writers, among whom Mr. James Joyce is the most notable, from that of their predecessors. They attempt to come closer to life, and to preserve more sincerely and exactly what interests and moves them, even if to do so they must discard most of the conventions which are commonly observed by the novelist. Let us record the atoms as they fall upon the mind in the order in which they fall, let us trace the pattern, however disconnected and incoherent in appearance, which each sight or incident scores upon the consciousness. Let us not take it for granted that life exists more fully in what is commonly thought big than in what is commonly thought small. Any one who has read *The Portrait of the Artist as a Young Man* or, what promises to be a far more interesting work, *Ulysses,* now appearing [1919] in the *Little Review,* will have hazarded some theory of this nature as to Mr. Joyce's intention. On our part, with such a fragment before us, it is hazarded rather than affirmed; but whatever the intention of the whole, there can be no question but that it is of the utmost sincerity and that the result, difficult or unpleasant as we may judge it, is undeniably important. In contrast with those whom we have called materialists, Mr. Joyce is spiritual; he is concerned at all costs to reveal the flickerings of that innermost flame which flashes its messages through the brain, and in order to preserve it he disregards with complete courage whatever seems to him adventitious, whether it be probability, or coherence, or any other of these signposts which for generations have served to support the imagination of a reader when called upon to imagine what he can neither touch nor see. The scene in the cemetery, for instance, with its brilliancy, its sordidity, its incoherence, its sudden lightning flashes of significance, does undoubtedly come so close to the quick of the mind that, on a first reading at any rate, it is difficult not to acclaim a masterpiece. If we want life itself, here surely we have it. Indeed, we find ourselves fumbling rather awkwardly if we try to say what else we wish, and for what reason a work of such originality yet fails to compare, for we must take high examples, with *Youth* or *The Mayor of Casterbridge*. It fails because of the comparative poverty of the writer's mind, we might say simply and have done with it. But it is possible to press a little further and wonder whether we may not refer our sense of being in a bright yet narrow room, confined and shut in, rather than enlarged and set free, to some limitation imposed by the method as well as by the mind. Is it the method that inhibits the creative power? Is it due to the method that we feel neither jovial nor magnanimous, but centred in a self which, in spite of its tremor of susceptibility, never embraces or creates what is outside itself and beyond? Does the emphasis laid, perhaps didactically, upon indecency, contribute to the effect of something angular and isolated? Or is it merely that in any effort of such originality it is much easier, for contemporaries especially, to feel what it lacks than to name what it gives? In any case it is a mistake to stand outside examining "methods". Any method is right, every method is right, that expresses what we wish to express, if we are writers; that brings us closer to the novelist's intention if we are readers. This method has the merit of bringing us closer to what we were prepared to call life itself; did not the reading of *Ulysses* suggest how much of life is excluded or ignored, and did it not come with a shock to open *Tristram Shandy* or even *Pendennis* and be by them convinced that there are not only other aspects of life, but more important ones into the bargain.

However this may be, the problem before the novelist at present, as we suppose it to have been in the past, is to contrive means of being free to set down what he chooses. He has to have the courage to say that what interests him is no longer "this" but "that": out of "that" alone must he construct his work. For the moderns "that", the point of interest, lies very likely in the dark places of psychology. At once, therefore, the accent falls a little differently; the emphasis is upon something hitherto ignored; at once a different outline of form becomes necessary, difficult for us to grasp, incomprehensible to our predecessors. No one but a modern, no one perhaps but a Russian, would have felt the interest of the situation which Tchekov has made into the short story which he calls "Gusev". Some Russian soldiers lie ill on board a ship which is taking them back to Russia. We are given a few scraps of their talk and some of their thoughts; then one of them dies and is carried away; the talk goes on among the others for a time, until Gusev himself dies, and looking "like a carrot or a radish" is thrown overboard. The emphasis is laid upon such unexpected places that at first it seems as if there were no emphasis at all; and then, as the eyes accustom themselves to twilight and discern the shapes of things in a room we see how complete the story is, how profound, and how truly in obedience to his vision Tchekov [Chekhov] has chosen this, that, and the other, and placed them together to compose something new. But it is impossible to say "this is comic", or "that is tragic", nor are we certain, since short stories, we have been taught, should be brief and conclusive, whether this, which is vague and inconclusive, should be called a short story at all.

The most elementary remarks upon modern English fiction can hardly avoid some mention of the Russian influence, and if the Russians are mentioned one runs the risk of feeling that to write of any fiction save theirs is waste of time. If we want understanding of the soul and heart where else shall we find it of comparable profundity? If we are sick of our own materialism the least considerable of their novelists has by right of birth a natural reverence for the human spirit. "Learn to make yourself akin to people. . . . But let this sympathy be not with the mind — for it is easy with the mind — but with the heart, with love towards them." In every great Russian writer we seem to discern the features of a saint, if sympathy for the sufferings of others, love towards them, endeavour to reach some goal worthy of the most exacting demands of the spirit constitute saintliness. It is the saint in them which confounds us with a feeling of our own irreligious triviality, and turns so many of our famous novels to tinsel and trickery. The conclusions of the Russian mind, thus comprehensive and compassionate, are inevitably, perhaps, of the utmost sadness. More accurately indeed we might speak of the inconclusiveness of the Russian mind. It is the sense that there is no answer, that if honestly examined life presents question after question which must be left to sound on and on after the story is over in hopeless interrogation that fills us with a deep, and finally it may be with a resentful, despair. They are right perhaps; unquestionably they see further than we do and without our gross impediments of vision. But perhaps we see something that escapes them, or why should this voice of protest mix itself with our gloom? The voice of protest is the voice of another and an ancient civilisation which seems to have bred in us the instinct to enjoy and fight rather than to suffer and understand. English fiction from Sterne to Meredith bears witness to our natural delight in humour and comedy, in the beauty of earth, in the activities of the intellect, and in the splendour of the body. But any deductions that we may draw from the comparison of two fictions so immeasurably far apart are futile save indeed as they flood us with a view of the infinite possibilities of the art and remind us that there is no limit to the horizon, and that nothing — no "method", no experiment, even of the wildest — is forbidden, but only falsity and pretence. "The proper stuff of fiction" does not exist; everything is the proper stuff of fiction, every feeling, every thought; every quality of brain and spirit is drawn upon; no perception comes amiss. And if we can imagine the art of fiction come alive and standing in our midst, she would undoubtedly bid us break her and bully her, as well as honour and love her, for so her youth is renewed and her sovereignty assured.

11
Inspiration

by Ralph Waldo Emerson

IT was Watt who told King George III. that he deal in an article of which kings were said to be fond, Power. 'Tis certain that the one thing we wish to know is, where power is to be bought. But we want a finer kind than that of commerce; and every reasonable man would give any price of house and land and future provision, for condensation, concentration and the recalling at will of high mental energy. Our money is only a second best. We would jump to buy power with it, that is, intellectual perception moving the will. That is first best. But we don't know where the shop is. If Watt knew, he forgot to tell us the number of the street. There are times when the intellect is so active that everything seems to run to meet it. Its supplies are found without much thought as to studies. Knowledge runs to the man, and the man runs to knowledge. In spring, when the snow melts, the maple-trees flow with sugar, and you cannot get tubs fast enough; but it is only for a few days. The hunter on the prairie, at the right season, has no need of choosing his ground; east, west, by the river, by the timber, he is everywhere near his game. But the favorable conditions are rather the exception than the rule.

The aboriginal man, in geology and in the dim light of Darwin's microscope, is not an engaging figure. We are very glad that he ate his fishes and snails and marrow-bones out of our sight and hearing, and that his doleful experiences were got through with so very long ago. They combed his mane, they pared his nails, cut off his tail, set him on end, sent him to school and made him pay taxes, before he could begin to write his sad story for the compassion or the repudiation of his descendants, who are all but unanimous to disown him. We must take him as we find him, — pretty well on in his education, and, in all our knowledge of him, an interesting creature with a will, an invention, an imagination, a conscience and an inextinguishable hope.

The Hunterian law of arrested development is not confined to vegetable and animal structure, but reaches the human intellect also. In the savage man, thought is infantile; and, in the civilized, unequal and ranging up and down a long scale. In the best races it is rare and imperfect. In happy moments it is reinforced, and carries out what were rude suggestions to larger scope and to clear and grand conclusions. The poet cannot see a natural phenomenon which does not express to him a correspondent fact in his mental experience; he is made aware of a power to carry on and complete the metamorphosis of natural into spiritual facts. Everything which we hear for the first time was expected by the mind: the newest discovery was expected. In the mind we call this enlarged power Inspiration. I believe that nothing great and lasting can be done except by inspiration, by leaning on the secret augury. The man's insight and power are interrupted and occasional; he can see and do this or that cheap task, at will, but it steads him not beyond. He is fain to make the ulterior step by mechanical means. It cannot so be done, That ulterior step is to be also by inspiration; if not through him, then by another man. Every real step is by what a poet called "lyrical glances," by lyrical facility, and never by main strength and ignorance. Years of mechanic toil will only seem to do it; it will not so be done.

Inspiration is like yeast. 'Tis no matter in which of half a dozen ways you procure the infection; you can apply one or the other equally well to your purpose, and get your loaf of bread. And every earnest workman, in whatever kind, knows some favorable conditions for his task. When I wish to write on any topic, 'tis of no consequence what kind of book or man gives me a hint or a motion, nor how far off that is from my topic.

Power is the first good. Rarey can tame a wild horse; but if he could give speed to a dull horse, were not that better? The toper finds, without asking, the road to the tavern, but the poet does not know the pitcher that holds his nectar. Every youth should know the way to prophecy as surely as the miller understands how to let on the water or the engineer the steam. A rush of thoughts is the only conceivable prosperity that can come to us. Fine clothes, equipages, villa, park, social consideration, cannot cover up real poverty and insignificance, from my own eyes or from others like mine

Thoughts let us into realities. Neither miracle nor magic nor any religious tradition, not the immortality of the private soul is incredible, after we have experienced an insight, a thought. I think it comes to some men but once in their life, sometimes a religious impulse, sometimes an intellectual insight. But what we want is consecutiveness. 'Tis with us a flash of light, then a long darkness, then a flash again. The separation of our days by sleep almost destroys identity. Could we but turn these fugitive sparkles into an astronomy of Copernican worlds! With most men, scarce a link of memory holds yesterday and to-day together. Their house and trade and families serve them as ropes to give a coarse continuity. But they have forgotten the thoughts of yesterday; they say today what occurs to them, and something else tomorrow. This insecurity of possession, this quick ebb of power,— as if life were a thunderstorm wherein you can see by a flash the horizon, and then cannot see your hand, — tantalizes us. We cannot make the inspiration consecutive. A glimpse, a point of view that by its brightness excludes the purview is granted, but no panorama. A fuller inspiration should cause the point to flow and become a line, should bend the line and complete the circle. To-day the electric machine will not work, no spark will pass; then presently the world is all a cat's back, all sparkle and shock. Sometimes there is no sea-fire, and again the sea is aglow to the horizon. Sometimes the Aeolian harp is dumb all day in the window, and again it is garrulous and tells all the secrets of the world. In June the morning is noisy with birds; in August they are already getting old and silent.

Hence arises the question, Are these moods in any degree within control? If we knew how to command them! But where is the Franklin with kite or rod for this fluid?— a Franklin who can draw off electricity from Jove himself, and convey it into the arts of life, inspire men, take them off their feet, withdraw them from the life of trifles and gain and comfort, and make the world transparent, so that they can read the symbols of Nature? What metaphysician has undertaken to enumerate the tonics of the torpid mind, the rules for the recovery of inspiration? That is least within control which is best in them. Of the modus of inspiration we have no knowledge. But in the experience of meditative men there is a certain agreement as to the conditions of reception. Plato, in his seventh Epistle, notes that the perception is only accomplished by long familiarity with the objects of intellect, and a life according to the things themselves. "Then a light, as if leaping from a fire, will on a sudden be enkindled in the soul, and will then itself nourish itself." He said again, "The man who is his own master knocks in vain at the doors of poetry." The artists must be sacrificed to their art. Like bees, they must put their lives into the sting they give. What is a man good for without enthusiasm? and what is enthusiasm but this daring of ruin for its object? There are thoughts beyond the reaches of our souls; we are not the less drawn to them. The moth flies into the flame of the lamp; and Swedenborg must solve the problems that haunt him, though he be crazed or killed.

There is genius as well in virtue as in intellect. 'Tis the doctrine of faith over works. The raptures of goodness are as old as history and new with this morning's sun. The legends of Arabia, Persia and India are of the same complexion as the Christian. Socrates, Mencius, Confucius, Zoroaster, — we recognize in all of them this ardor to solve the hints of thought.

I hold that ecstasy will be found normal, or only an example on a higher plane of the same gentle gravitation by which stones fall and rivers run. Experience identifies. Shakspeare seems to you miraculous; but the wonderful juxtapositions, parallelisms, transfers, which his genius effected, were all to him locked together as links of a chain, and the mode precisely as conceivable and familiar to higher intelligence as the index-making of the literary hack. The result of the hack is inconceivable to the type-setter who waits for it.

We must prize our own youth. Later, we want heat to execute our plans: the good will, the knowledge, the whole armory of means are all present, but a certain heat that once used not to fail, refuses its office, and all is vain until this capricious fuel is supplied. It seems a semi-animal heat; as if tea, or wine, or sea-air, or mountains, or a genial companion, or a new thought suggested in book or conversation could fire the train, wake the fancy and the clear perception. Pit-coal, — where to find it? 'Tis of no use that your engine is made like a watch, — that you are a good workman, and know how to drive it, if there is no coal. We are waiting until some tyrannous idea emerging out of heaven shall seize and bereave us of this liberty with which we are falling abroad. Well, we have the same hint or suggestion, day by day. "I am not," says the man, "at the top of my condition to-day, but the favorable hour will come when I can command all my powers, and when that will be easy to do which is at this moment impossible." See how the passions augment our force,— anger, love, ambition — sometimes sympathy, and the expectation of men. Garrick said that on the stage his great paroxysms surprised himself as much as his audience. If this is true on this low plane, it is true on the higher. Swedenborg's genius was the perception of the doctrine that "The Lord flows into the spirits of angels and of men;" and all poets have signalized their consciousness of rare moments when they were superior to themselves,— when a light, a freedom, a power came to them which lifted them to performances far better than they could reach at other times; so that a religious poet once told me that he valued his poems, not because they were his, but because they were not. He thought the angels brought them to him.

Jacob Behmen{1} said: "Art has not wrote here, nor was there any time to consider how to set it punctually down according to the right understanding of the letters, but all was ordered according to the direction of the spirit, which often went on haste,— so that the penman's hand, by reason he was not accustomed to it, did often shake. And, though I could have written in a more accurate, fair and plain manner, the burning fire often forced forward with speed, and the hand and pen must hasten directly after it, for it comes and goes as a sudden shower. In one quarter of an hour I saw and knew more than if I had been many years together at an university."

The depth of the notes which we accidentally sound on the strings of Nature is out of all proportion to our taught and ascertained faculty, and might teach us what strangers and novices we are, vagabond in this universe of pure power, to which we have only the smallest key. Herrick said—

> "'Tis not every day that I
> Fitted am to prophesy;
> No, but when the spirit fills
> The fantastic panicles,
> Full of fire, then I write
> As the Godhead doth indite.
> Thus enraged, my lines are hurled,
> Like the Sibyl's, through the world:
> Look how next the holy fire
> Either slakes, or doth retire;
> So the fancy cools.— till when
> That brave spirit comes again."

Bonaparte said:
"There is no man more Pusillanimous than I, when I make a military plan. I magnify all the dangers, and all the possible mischances. I am in an agitation utterly painful. That does not prevent me from appearing quite serene to the persons who surround me. I am like a woman with child, and when my resolution is taken, all is forgot except whatever can make it succeed."

There are, to be sure, certain risks in this presentiment of the decisive perception, as in the use of ether or alcohol:

> "Great wits to madness nearly are allied;
> Both serve to make our poverty our pride."

Aristotle said: "No great genius was ever without some mixture of madness, nor can anything grand or superior to the voice of common mortals be spoken except by the agitated soul." We might say of these memorable moments of life that we were in them, not they in us. We found our selves by happy fortune in an illuminated portion of meteorous zone, and passed out of it again, so aloof was it from any will of ours. "It is a principle of war," said Napoleon, "that when you can use the lightning it is better than cannon."

How many sources of inspiration can we count? As many as our affinities. But to a practical purpose we may reckon a few of these.

1. Health is the first muse, comprising the magical benefits of air, landscape and bodily exercise, on the mind. The Arabs say that "Allah does not count from life the days spent in the chase," that is, those are thrown in. Plato thought "exercise would almost cure a guilty conscience." Sydney Smith said: "You will never break down in a speech on the day when you have walked twelve miles."

I honor health as the first muse, and sleep as the condition of health. Sleep benefits mainly by the sound health it produces; incidentally also by dreams, into whose farrago a divine lesson is sometimes slipped. Life is in short cycles or periods; we are quickly tired, but we have rapid rallies. A man is spent by his work, starved, prostrate; he will not lift his hand to save his life; he can never think more. He sinks into deep sleep and wakes with renewed youth, with hope, courage, fertile in resources, and keen for daring adventure.

"Sleep is like death, and after sleep
The world seems new begun:
White thoughts stand luminous and firm,
Like statues in the sun;
Refreshed from supersensuous founts,
The soul to clearer vision mounts."

A man must be able to escape from his cares and fears, as well as from hunger and want of sleep; so that another Arabian proverb has its coarse truth: "When the belly is full, it says to the head, Sing, fellow!" The perfection of writing is when mind and body are both in key; when the mind finds perfect obedience in the body. And wine, no doubt, and all fine food, as of delicate fruits, furnish some elemental wisdom. And the fire, too, as it burns in the chimney; for I fancy that my logs, which have grown so long in sun and wind by Walden, are a kind of muses. So of all the particulars of health and exercise and fit nutriment and tonics. Some people will tell you there is a great deal of poetry and fine sentiment in a chest of tea.

2. The experience of writing letters is one of the keys to the modus of inspiration. When we have ceased for a long time to have any fulness of thoughts that once made a diary a joy as well as a necessity, and have come to believe that an image or a happy turn of expression is no longer at our command, in writing a letter to a friend we may find that we rise to thought and to a cordial power of expression that costs no effort, and it seems to us that this facility may be indefinitely applied and resumed. The wealth of the mind in this respect of seeing is like that of a looking-glass, which is never

tired or worn by any multitude of objects which it reflects, You may carry it all round the world, it is ready and perfect as ever for new millions.

3. Another consideration, though it will not so much interest young men, will cheer the heart of older scholars, namely that there is diurnal and secular rest. As there is this daily renovation of sensibility, so it sometimes if rarely happens that after a season of decay or eclipse, darkening months or years, the faculties revive to their fullest force. One of the best facts I know in metaphysical science is Niebuhr's joyful record that after his genius for interpreting history had failed him for several years, this divination returned to him. As this rejoiced me, so does Herbert's poem *The Flower.* His health had broken down early, he had lost his muse, and in this poem he says:

"And now in age I bud again,
After so many deaths I live and write:
I once more smell the dew and rain,
And relish versing: O my only light,
It cannot be
That I am he
On whom thy tempests fell all night."

His poem called *The Forerunners* also has supreme interest. I understand *The Harbingers* to refer to the signs of age and decay which he detects in himself, not only in his constitution, but in his fancy and his facility and grace in writing verse; and he signalizes his delight in this skill, and his pain that the Herricks, Lovelaces and Marlowes, or whoever else, should use the like genius in language to sensual purpose, and consoles himself that his own faith and the divine life in him remain to him unchanged, unharmed.

4. The power of the will is sometimes sublime; and what is will for, if it cannot help us in emergencies? Seneca says of an almost fatal sickness that befell him, "The thought of my father, who could not have sustained such a blow as my death, restrained me; I commanded myself to live." Goethe said to Eckermann, "I work more easily when the barometer is high than when it is low. Since I know this, I endeavor, when the barometer is low, to counteract the injurious effect by greater exertion, and my attempt is successful."

"To the persevering mortal the blessed immortals are swift." Yes, for they know how to give you in one moment the solution of the riddle you have pondered for months. "Had I not lived with Mirabeau," says Dumont, "I never should have known all that can be done in one day, or, rather, in an interval of twelve hours. A day to him was of more value than a week or a month to others. To-morrow to him was not the same impostor as to most others."

5. Plutarch affirms that "souls are naturally endowed with the faculty of prediction, and the chief cause that excites this faculty and virtue is a certain temperature of air and winds." My anchorite thought it "sad that atmospheric influences should bring to our dust the communion of the soul with the Infinite." But I am glad that the atmosphere should be an excitant, glad to find the dull rock itself to be deluged with Deity, to be theist, Christian, poetic. The fine influences of the morning few can explain, but all will admit. Goethe acknowledges them in the poem in which he dislodges the nightingale from her place as Leader of the Muses:

MUSAGETES

"Often in deep midnights
I called on the sweet muses.
No dawn shines,
And no day will appear:
But at the right hour
The lamp brings me pious light,
That it, instead of Aurora or Phoebus,
May enliven my quiet industry.
But they left me lying in sleep
Dull, and not to be enlivened,
And after every late morning
Followed unprofitable days.

When now the Spring stirred,
I said to the nightingales:
'Dear nightingales, trill
Early, O, early before my lattice,
Wake me out of the deep sleep
Which mightily chains the young man.'
But the love-filled singers
Poured by night before my window
Their sweet melodies,—
Kept awake my dear soul,

Roused tender new longings
In my lately touched bosom,
And so the night passed,

And Aurora found me sleeping:
Yea, hardly did the sun wake me.
At last it has become summer,
And at the first glimpse of morning
The busy early fly stings me
Out of my sweet slumber.
Unmerciful she returns again:
When often the half-awake victim
Impatiently drives her off.
She calls hither the unscrupulous sisters,
And from my eyelids
Sweet sleep must depart.

Vigorous, I spring from my couch,
Seek the beloved Muses,
Find them in the beech grove.
Pleased to receive me;
And I thank the annoying insect
For many a golden hour.
Stand, then, for me, ye tormenting creatures,
Highly praised by the poet
As the true Musagetes."

The French have a proverb to the effect that not the day only, but all things have their morning, —"*Il n'y a que le matin en routes choses.*" And it is a primal rule to defend your morning, to keep all its dews on, and with fine foresight to relieve it from any jangle of affairs—even from the question, Which task? I remember a capital prudence of old President Quincy, who told me that he never went to bed at night until he had laid out the studies for the next morning. I believe that in our good days a well-ordered mind has a new thought awaiting it every morning. And hence, eminently thoughtful men, from the time of Pythagoras down, have insisted on an hour of solitude every day, to meet their own mind and learn what oracle it has to impart. If a new view of life or mind gives us joy, so does new arrangement. I don't know but we take as much delight, in finding the right place for an old observation, as in a new thought.

6. Solitary converse with Nature; for thence are ejaculated sweet and dreadful words never uttered in libraries. Ah! the spring days, the summer dawns, the October woods! I confide that my reader knows these delicious secrets, has perhaps

> Slighted Minerva's learned tongue,
> But leaped with joy when on the wind the shell
> of Clio rung.

Are you poetical, impatient of trade, tired of labor and affairs? Do you want Monadnoc, Agiocochook, or Helvellyn, or Plinlimmon, dear to English song, in your closet? Caerleon, Provence, Ossian and Cadwallon? Tie a couple of strings across a board and set it in your window, and you have an instrument which no artist's harp can rival. It needs no instructed ear; if you have sensibility, it admits you to sacred interiors; it has the sadness of Nature, yet, at the changes, tones of triumph and festal notes ringing out all measures of loftiness. "Did you never observe," says Gray, "'while rocking winds are piping loud,' that pause, as the gust is recollecting itself, and rising upon the ear in a shrill and plaintive note, like the swell of an Aeolian harp? I do assure you there is nothing in the world so like the voice of a spirit." Perhaps you can recall a delight like it, which spoke to the eye, when you have stood by a lake in the woods in summer, and saw where little flaws of wind whip spots or patches of still water into fleets of ripples,—so sudden, so slight, so spiritual, that it was more like the rippling of the Aurora Borealis at night than any spectacle of day.

7. But the solitude of Nature is not so essential as solitude of habit. I have found my advantage in going in summer to a country inn, in winter to a city hotel, with a task which would not prosper at home. I thus secured a more absolute seclusion; for it is almost impossible for a housekeeper who is in the country a small farmer, to exclude interruptions and even necessary orders, though I bar out by system all I can, and resolutely omit, to my constant damage, all that can be omitted. At home, the day is cut into short strips. In the hotel, I have no hours to keep, no visits to make or receive, and I command an astronomic leisure. I forget rain, wind, cold and heat. At home, I remember in my library the wants of the farm, and have all too much sympathy. I envy the abstraction of some scholars I have known, who could sit on a curbstone in State Street, put up their back, and solve their problem. I have more womanly eyes. All the conditions must be right

for my success, slight as that is. What untunes is as bad as what cripples or stuns me. Novelty, surprise, change of scene, refresh the artist, —"break up the tiresome old roof of heaven into new forms," as Hafiz said. The seashore and the taste of two metals in contact, and our enlarged powers in the presence, or rather at the approach and at the departure of a friend, and the mixture of lie in truth, and the experience of poetic creativeness which is not found in staying at home nor yet in travelling, but in transitions from one to the other, which must therefore be adroitly managed to present as much transitional surface as possible,— these are the types or conditions of this power. "A ride near the sea, a sail near the shore," said the ancient. So Montaigne travelled with his books, but did not read in them. "La Nature aime les croisements," says Fourier. {2}

I know there is room for whims here; but in regard to some apparent trifles there is great agreement as to their annoyance. And the machine with which we are dealing is of such an inconceivable delicacy that whims also must be respected. Fire must lend its aid. We not only want time, but warm time. George Sand says, "I have no enthusiasm for Nature which the slightest chill will not I instantly destroy." And I remember Thoreau, with his robust will, yet found certain trifles disturbing the delicacy of that health which composition exacted,—namely, the slightest irregularity, even to the drinking too much water on the preceding day. Even a steel pen is a nuisance to some writers. Some of us may remember, years ago, in the English journals, the petition, signed by Carlyle, Browning, Tennyson, Dickens and other writers in London, against the license of the organ-grinders, who infested the streets near their houses, to levy on them blackmail.

Certain localities, as mountaintops, the seaside, the shores of rivers and rapid brooks, natural parks of oak and pine, where the ground is smooth and unencumbered, are excitants of the muse. Every artist knows well some favorite retirement. And yet the experience of some good artists has taught them to prefer the smallest and plainest chamber, with one chair and table and with no outlook, to these picturesque liberties. William Blake said, "Natural objects always did and do weaken, deaden and obliterate imagination in me." And Sir Joshua Reynolds had no pleasure in Richmond; he used to say "the human face was his landscape." These indulgences are to be used with great caution. Allston rarely left his studio by day. An old friend took him, one fine afternoon, a spacious circuit into the country, and he painted two or three pictures as the fruits of that drive, But he made it a rule not to go to the city on two consecutive days. One was rest; more was lost time. The times of force must be well husbanded, and the wise student will remember the prudence of Sir Tristram in Morte d'Arthur, who, having received from the fairy an enchantment of six hours of growing strength every day, took care to fight in the hours when his strength increased; since from noon to night his strength abated. What prudence again does every artist, every scholar need in the security of his easel or his desk! These must be remote from the work of the house, and from all knowledge of the feet that come and go therein. Allston, it is said, had two or three rooms in different parts of Boston, where he could not be found. For the delicate muses lose their head if their attention is once diverted. Perhaps if you were successful abroad in talking and dealing with men, you would not come back to your book-shelf and your task. When the spirit chooses you for its scribe to publish some commandment, it makes you odious to men and men odious to you, and you shall accept that loathsomeness with joy. The moth must fly to the lamp, and you must solve those questions though you die.

8. Conversation, which, when it is best, is a series of intoxications. Not Aristotle, not Kant or Hegel, but conversation, is the right metaphysical professor. This is the true school of philosophy,—this the college where you learn what thoughts are, what powers lurk in those fugitive gleams, and what becomes of them; how they make history. A wise man goes to this game to play upon others and to be played upon, and at least as curious to know what can be drawn from himself as what can be drawn from them. For, in discourse with a friend, our thought, hitherto wrapped in our consciousness, detaches itself, and allows itself to be seen as a thought, in a manner as new and entertaining to us as to our companions. For provocation of thought, we use ourselves and use each other. Some perceptions—I think the best—are granted to the single soul; they come from the depth and go to the depth and are the permanent and controlling ones. Others it takes two to find. We must be warmed by the fire of sympathy, to be brought into the right conditions and angles of vision. Conversation; for intellectual activity is contagious. We are emulous. If the tone of the companion is higher than ours, we delight in rising to it. 'Tis a historic observation that a writer must find an audience up to his thought, or he will no longer care to impart it, but will sink to their level or be silent. Homer said, "When two come together, one apprehends before the other;" but it is because one thought well that the other thinks better: and two men of good mind will excite each other's activity, each attempting still to cap the other's thought. In enlarged conversation we have suggestions that require new ways of living, new books, new men, new arts and sciences. By sympathy, each opens to the eloquence, and begins to see with the eyes of his mind. We were all lonely, thoughtless; and now a principle appears to all: we see new relations, many truths; every mind seizes them as they pass; each catches by the mane one of these strong coursers like horses of the prairie, and rides up and down in the world of

the intellect. We live day by day under the illusion that it is the fact or event that imports, whilst really it is not that which signifies, but the use we put it to, or what we think of it. We esteem nations important, until we discover that a few individuals much more concern us; then, later, that it is not at last a few individuals, or any sacred heroes, but the lowliness, the outpouring, the large equality to truth of a single mind,—as if in the narrow walls of a human heart the whole realm of truth, the world of morals, the tribunal by which the universe is judged, found room to exist.

9. New poetry; by which I mean chiefly, old poetry that is new to the reader. I have heard from persons who had practice in rhyming, that it was sufficient to set them on writing verses, to read any original poetry. What is best in literature is the affirming, prophesying, spermatic words of men-making poets. Only that is poetry which cleanses and mans me.

Words used in a new sense and figuratively, dart a delightful lustre; and every word admits a new use, and hints ulterior meanings. We have not learned the law of the mind,—cannot control and domesticate at will the high states of contemplation and continuous thought. "Neither by sea nor by land," said Pindar, "canst thou find the way to the Hyperboreans;" neither by idle wishing, nor by rule of three or rule of thumb. Yet I find a mitigation or solace by providing always a good book for my journeys, as Horace or Martial or Goethe, —some book which lifts me quite out of prosaic surroundings, and from which I draw some lasting knowledge. A Greek epigram out of the anthology, a verse of Herrick or Lovelace, are in harmony both with sense and spirit.

You shall not read newspapers, nor politics, nor novels, nor Montaigne, nor the newest French book. You may read Plutarch, Plato, Plotinus, Hindoo mythology and ethics. You may read Chaucer, Shakspeare, Ben Jonson, Milton, and Milton's prose as his verse; read Collins and Gray; read Hafiz and the Trouveurs; nay, Welsh and British mythology of Arthur, and (in your ear) Ossian; fact-books, which all geniuses prize as raw material, and as antidote to verbiage and false poetry. Fact-books, if the facts be well and thoroughly told, are much more nearly allied to poetry than many books are that are written in rhyme. Only our newest knowledge works as a source of inspiration and thought, as only the outmost layer of Tiber on the tree. Books of natural science, especially those written by the ancients,—geography, botany, agriculture, explorations of the sea, of meteors, of astronomy,—all the better if written without literary aim or ambition. Every book is good to read which sets the reader in a working mood. The deep book, no matter how remote the subject, helps us best.

Neither are these all the sources, nor can I name all. The receptivity is rare. The occasions or predisposing circumstances I could never tabulate; but now one, now another landscape, form, color, or companion, or perhaps one kind of sounding word or syllable, "strikes the electric chain with which we are darkly bound," and it is impossible to detect and wilfully repeat the fine conditions to which we have owed our happiest frames of mind. The day is good in which we have had the most perceptions. The analysis is the more difficult, because poppy-leaves are strewn when a generalization is made; for I can never remember the circumstances to which I owe it, so as to repeat the experiment or put myself in the conditions:—

"'Tis the most difficult of tasks to keep
Heights which the soul is competent to gain."

I value literary biography for the hints it furnishes from so many scholars, in so many countries, of what hygiene, what ascetic, what gymnastic, what social practices their experience suggested and approved. They are, for the most part, men who needed only a little wealth. Large estates, political relations, great hospitalities, would have been impediments to them. They are men whom a book could entertain, a new thought intoxicate and hold them prisoners for years perhaps. Aubrey and Burton and Wood tell me incidents which I find not insignificant.

These are some hints towards what is in all education a chief necessity,— the right government, or, shall I not say? the right obedience to the powers of the human soul. Itself is the dictator: the mind itself the awful oracle. All our power, all our happiness consists in our reception of its hints, which ever become clearer and grander as they are obeyed.

Notes to Emerson's *Inspiration*

{1} Jacob Behmen was a Christian mystic, born in Germany, who lived from 1575 to 1624. His name has been spelled in various ways, including Jakob Böhme, and Jakob Boehme.

{2} The saying of Fourier: *"La Nature aime les croisements,"* ... might be rendered into English as: "Nature likes the intersections." (MP)

12
"Dollars Damn Me!"
A Letter to Hawthorne (June 1851)

by Herman Melville

My dear Hawthorne,—I should have been rumbling down to you in my pine-board chariot a long time ago, were it not that for some weeks past I have been more busy than you can well imagine,—out of doors,—building and patching and tinkering away in all directions. Besides, I had my crops to get in,—corn and potatoes (I hope to show you some famous ones by and by),—and many other things to attend to, all accumulating upon this one particular season. I work myself; and at night my bodily sensations are akin to those I have so often felt before, when a hired man, doing my day's work from sun to sun. But I mean to continue visiting you until you tell me that my visits are both supererogatory and superfluous. With no son of man do I stand upon any etiquette or ceremony, except the Christian ones of charity and honesty. I am told, my fellow-man, that there is an aristocracy of the brain. Some men have boldly advocated and asserted it. Schiller seems to have done so, though I don't know much about him. At any rate, it is true that there have been those who, while earnest in behalf of political equality, still accept the intellectual estates. And I can well perceive, I think, how a man of superior mind can, by its intense cultivation bring himself, as it were, into a certain spontaneous aristocracy of feeling,—exceedingly nice and fastidious,—similar to that which, in an English Howard, conveys a torpedo-fish thrill at the slightest contact with a social plebeian. So, when you see or hear of my ruthless democracy on all sides, you may possibly feel a touch of a shrink, or something of that sort. It is but nature to be shy of a mortal who boldly declares that a thief in jail is as honorable a personage as Gen. George Washington. This is ludicrous. But Truth is the silliest thing under the sun. Try to get a living by the Truth—and go to the Soup Societies. Heavens! Let any clergyman try to preach the Truth from its very stronghold, the pulpit, and they would ride him out of his church on his own pulpit bannister. It can hardly be doubted that all Reformers are bottomed upon the truth, more or less; and to the world at large are not reformers almost universally laughing-stocks? Why so? Truth is ridiculous to men. Thus easily in my room here do I, conceited and garrulous, reverse the test of my Lord Shaftesbury.

It seems an inconsistency to assert unconditional democracy in all things, and yet confess a dislike to all mankind—in the mass. But not so. But it's an endless sermon,—no more of it. I began by saying that the reason I have not been to Lenox is this,—in the evening I feel completely done up, as the phrase is, and incapable of the long jolting to get to your house and back. In a week or so, I go to New York, to bury myself in a third-story room, and work and slave on my "Whale" while it is driving through the press. That is the only way I can finish it now,—I am so pulled hither and thither by circumstances. The calm, the coolness, the silent grass-growing mood in which a man ought always to compose,—that, I fear, can seldom be mine. Dollars damn me; and the malicious Devil is forever grinning in upon me, holding the door ajar. My dear Sir, a presentiment is on me,—I shall at last be worn out and perish, like an old nutmeg-grater, grated to pieces by the constant attrition of the wood, that is, the nutmeg. What I feel most moved to write, that is banned,—it will not pay. Yet, altogether, write the other way I cannot. So the product is a final hash, and all my books are botches. I'm rather sore, perhaps, in this letter; but see my hand!— four blisters on this palm, made by hoes and hammers within the last few days. It is a rainy morning; so I am indoors, and all work suspended. I feel cheerfully disposed, and therefore I write a little bluely. Would the Gin were here! If ever, my dear Hawthorne, in the eternal times that are to come, you and I shall sit down in Paradise, in some little shady corner by ourselves; and if we shall by any means be able to smuggle a basket of champagne there (I won't believe in a Temperance Heaven), and if we shall then cross our celestial legs in the celestial grass that is forever tropical, and strike our glasses and our heads together, till both musically ring in concert, then, O my dear fellow-mortal, how shall we pleasantly discourse of all the things manifold which now so distress us,—when all the earth shall be but a reminiscence, yea, its final dissolution an antiquity. Then shall songs be composed as when wars are over; humorous, comic songs, —"Oh, when I lived in that queer little hole called the world," or, "Oh, when I toiled and sweated below," or, "Oh, when I knocked and was knocked in the fight"—yes, let us fool, forward to such things. Let us swear that, though now we sweat, yet it is because of the dry heat which is indispensable to the nourishment of the vine which is to bear the grapes that are to give us the champagne hereafter.

But I was talking about the "Whale." As the fishermen say, "he's in his flurry" when I left him some three weeks ago. I'm going to take him by his jaw, however, before long, and finish him up in some fashion or other. What's the use of elaborating what, in its very essence, is so short-lived as a modern book? Though I wrote the Gospels in this century, I should die in the gutter.—I talk all about myself, and this is selfishness and egotism. Granted. But how help it? I am writing to you; I know little about you, but something about myself. So I write about myself,—at least, to you. Don't trouble yourself, though, about writing; and don't trouble yourself about visiting; and when you do visit, don't trouble yourself about talking. I will do all the writing and visiting and talking myself.—By the way, in the last "Dollar Magazine" I read "The Unpardonable Sin." He was a sad fellow, that Ethan Brand. I have no doubt you are by this time responsible for many a shake and tremor of the tribe of "general readers." It is a frightful poetical creed that the cultivation of the brain eats out the heart. But it's my prose opinion that in most cases, in those men who have fine brains and work them well, the heart extends down to hams. And though you smoke them with the fire of tribulation, yet, like veritable hams, the head only gives the richer and the better flavor. I stand for the heart. To the dogs with the head! I had rather be a fool with a heart, than Jupiter Olympus with his head. The reason the mass of men fear God, and at bottom dislike Him, is because they rather distrust His heart, and fancy Him all brain like a watch. (You perceive I employ a capital initial in the pronoun referring to the Deity; don't you think there is a slight dash of flunkeyism in that usage?) Another thing. I was in New York for four-and-twenty hours the other day, and saw a portrait of N. H. And I have seen and heard many flattering (in a publisher's point of view) allusions to the "Seven Gables." And I have seen "Tales," and "A New Volume" announced, by N. H. So upon the whole, I say to myself, this N. H. is in the ascendant. My dear Sir, they begin to patronize. All Fame is patronage. Let me be infamous: there is no patronage in that. What "reputation" H. M. has is horrible. Think of it! To go down to posterity is bad enough, any way; but to go down as a "man who lived among the cannibals"! When I speak of posterity, in reference to myself, I only mean the babies who will probably be born in the moment immediately ensuing upon my giving up the ghost. I shall go down to some of them, in all likelihood. "Typee" will be given to them, perhaps, with their gingerbread. I have come to regard this matter of Fame as the most transparent of all vanities. I read Solomon more and more, and every time see deeper and deeper and unspeakable meanings in him. I did not think of Fame, a year ago, as I do now. My development has been all within a few years past. I am like one of those seeds taken out of the Egyptian Pyramids, which, after being three thousand years a seed and nothing but a seed, being planted in English soil, it developed itself, grew to greenness, and then fell to mould. So I. Until I was twenty-five, I had no development at all. From my twenty-fifth year I date my life. Three weeks have scarcely passed, at any time between then and now, that I have not unfolded within myself. But I feel that I am now come to the inmost leaf of the bulb, and that shortly the flower must fall to the mould. It seems to me now that Solomon was the truest man who ever spoke, and yet that he a little managed the truth with a view to popular conservatism; or else there have been many corruptions and interpolations of the text—In reading some of Goethe's sayings, so worshipped by his votaries, I came across this, "Live in the all." That is to say, your separate identity is but a wretched one,—good; but get out of yourself, spread and expand yourself, and bring to yourself the tinglings of life that are felt in the flowers and the woods, that are felt in the planets Saturn and Venus, and the Fixed Stars. What nonsense! Here is a fellow with a raging toothache. "My dear boy," Goethe says to him, "you are sorely afflicted with that tooth; but you must live in the all, and then you will be happy!" As with all great genius, there is an immense deal of flummery in Goethe, and in proportion to my own contact with him, a monstrous deal of it in me.

H. Melville

P. S. "Amen!" saith Hawthorne.

N.B. This "all" feeling, though, there is some truth in. You must often have felt it, lying on the grass on a warm summer's day. Your legs seem to send out shoots into the earth. Your hair feels like leaves upon your head. This is the all feeling. But what plays mischief with the truth is that men will insist upon the universal application of a temporary feeling or opinion.

P.S. You must not fail to admire my discretion in paying the postage on this letter.

13
Balzac's Advice to Artists

by Honore de Balzac
(translation by Michael Pastore)

The solution to the artist's overwhelming problem is to be found only in constant work. In this way, the technical matters will be thoroughly mastered, so that the artist is free for the great struggle to imbue the work with vitality, and the essence of his inner life. If Paganini, who expressed his whole soul through the strings of his violin, spent three days without practicing, he lost what he called the rapport with his instrument, meaning the sympathy between the wooden frame, the strings, the bow, and himself. If he had lost this alliance, he would have been no more than an ordinary player on the street.

Constant work is the law of art, as it is the law of life, for art is idealized creation. Therefore, the great artists and sublime poets never wait for commissions or for buyers. They are ceaselessly creating—today, tomorrow, always. The result is the habit of work, and the profound understanding of the work's difficulties, which keep them in close connection with the Muse and her creative powers. Canova lived in his studio, as Voltaire lived in his study; and so must Homer and Phidias have lived.

[And Begin Working Now ...]

"Then, I hope you mean to work, my dear treasure," said Hortense.
"Yes, of course," said the artist. "I will begin tomorrow."
"Tomorrow is our ruin!" said his smiling wife.

14
What is Editing? and
Why Does It Make a Difference?

by Michael Pastore

Leo Tolstoy worked for five years (1864–1869) on his great novel, *War and Peace.* It contains more than 563,600 words. Tolstoy's editor, his 20-year-old-wife Sonya, copied the massive manuscript by hand seven times. In her autobiography, Sonya wrote:

> "Often in copying I was surprised and could not understand why passages that to me seemed so beautiful had been changed or eliminated, and I always rejoiced when they were restored. I was so absorbed in the work of copying, that I frequently sensed the rough spots, such as an excessive use of the same word or a long sentence in which punctuation had to be changed to bring out the thought more clearly. I called my husband's attention to them. Sometimes my comments delighted him, or else he explained why he had to do it that way, and said that details were not important, and only the general effect counted ... In copying, I at times took it on myself to call his attention to, and even ask him to eliminate, anything that seemed unfit to be read by young people. For example, the scenes in War and Peace built around the cynical and beautiful Helen — and Lev often agreed. Frequently, as I copied the beautiful poetical passages in my husband's writings, I cried, not only because I was moved, but also from artistic exaltation that I shared with the author."

As more books and ebooks are published every year, publishers and authors should say: "Good editing is one of our highest priorities." Sadly, the opposite is happening: editing is vanishing like Arctic ice. Large publishers are cutting down on their in-house and freelance editing budgets; and too many self-published authors — who need it most — hardly edit their books at all.

The very first line of a novel offered for sale as an ebook began this way:

"His hand creeped up my naked thigh like a beast of pray."

Although the author has invented a new genre — the erotic-religious — that opening gaffe discouraged me from reading more.

The decline in print-book editing was first acknowledged in a 1998 *New York Times* article by Doreen Carvajal, titled: 'The More the Books, The Fewer the Editors: As Publishing Pressures Rise, So Do Errors.'

The article states that in the past 10 years there are fewer professional editors: a sixteen percent drop. More books are being published, and there is now a shorter time from manuscript to published book: sometimes as little as 4 to 6 months, whereas the previous time span was 9 months. Modern editors are playing too many roles in addition to sitting at the desk and editing.

One cause of the problem is obvious: books are being written and produced too quickly. Another cause is also clear: Editing is unappreciated and misunderstood.

What are the varieties of editing? The experts themselves disagree. Look how the *Chicago Manual of Style* (CMOS) 15th edition, defines editing, on page 71, section 2.48:

"Manuscript editing as opposed to developmental editing. Manuscript editing, also called copy editing or line editing, ... requires attention to every word in a manuscript, a thorough knowledge of the style to be followed ... "

According to CMOS (which, it should be noted well, is concerned with editing nonfiction works only) in the passage above, manuscript editing is synonymous with copyediting. Yet another much-trusted source clearly disagrees. This is how *Merriam-Webster's Manual for Writers & Editors* (revised edition, 1998, page 276) defines editing:

"This higher-level editing is often known as manuscript editing or line editing, names which distinguish it from what is known as copyediting."

Even the *Chicago Manual of Style* nods: Merriam and Webster are correct. Manuscript editing and copyediting are two distinct processes. Stepping back, the complete editorial picture may be divided into six phases.

On the following page, a chart illustrates these six phases of editing a book. Note that between phase 1 and phase 2, the author will have written the book's first draft.

The Six Phases of Book Editing

Each of the six phases of book editing addresses unique problems, and requires an editor with specific skills. Between phases 1 and 2, the writer has written the first draft of the book.

	The Six Phases of Book Editing
1	Book Planning, or Developmental Editing
	[Author writes the first draft]
2	Revising / Rewriting
3	Manuscript Editing
4	Style Editing
5	Copyediting
6	Proofreading

The Six Phases of Book Editing

Although there is a great deal of overlap regarding who will perform the work, the six phases of editing are easily distinguishable and distinct.

1. Book Planning or Developmental Editing.

If the writer is working alone she needs to plan the book; if this planning is done at a large publishing house it is called Developmental Editing. For nonfiction works, this first phase of the book tackles the largest pre-writing questions: What is the book about? Who is it written for? How large will the book be, and how much emphasis will be given to which subtopics? ... For fiction, each writer has her own planning process that will cover Characters, Plot and Structure, Voice and Tone, Themes and Ideas, and much more.

2. Revising/Rewriting.

After the first draft has been written, the writer reads the work, aloud if he likes to hear his own voice. In this phase he makes changes in substance and style. In revising/rewriting, the author often works without specific changes in mind: revising is somewhat spontaneous. Editing is different from rewriting: editors look for well-known problems and features.

3. Manuscript Editing (also called: Substantive Editing)

After the book has been written and revised, this phase analyzes and then fixes the largest and most difficult problems. These include issues such as scope and intensity (whether to expand or cut specific sections); organization (where things go, and how content might be rearranged); tone; and making ideas and arguments clearer and more profound.

4. Style Editing

Paragraphs and sentences that are awkward and unclear need to be rewritten. This work should be called style editing. In practice, it is often performed by either the manuscript editor or the copyeditor, or one of these will point out problems to the author and ask the author to do it. Style-editing decisions are much less significant than manuscript editing questions, but they demand more creativity and writing skill than copyediting. What do style editors do? Make things clearer, more graceful, more concise. They might select the right word, not the nearly right word. They might change a sentence from the passive voice to the active voice. They might omit needless words, make the paragraph the unit of composition (one paragraph to each topic), or rearrange words in a sentence so that the end of the sentence carries the most significant words.

5. Copyediting

The main work of the copyeditor is to correct the manuscript for errors and inconsistencies. Copyediting is concerned with grammar, spelling, usage, punctuation, capitalization, abbreviation, checking that facts are accurate, and making sure that the manuscript is consistent ("Sam Smith" is not "Sam Smyth"; the "State of New York" does not appear later as "New York State"). Copyeditors — who do many different jobs and are underpaid — might also be responsible for checking references, bibliographies, and footnotes; testing internal and external hyperlinks (in electronic documents); and evaluating the manuscript for legal problems such as libel, copyright infringement, plagiarism, and bias about race, age, or sex.

6. Proofreading

When the "page proofs" are ready, proofreaders are called in like baseball relief pitchers to save the book from humiliating mistakes. Proofreading comprises the final check for typographical and spelling errors, faulty page numbering, missing pages, formatting features (e.g., Are all the headings in the same font size and style?), and consistency throughout the work.

What do manuscript editors do?

Manuscript editors work on these problems:

1. Planning. Does the work have a clear plan and a meaningful underlying structure?

2. Audience. Who will be interested in the book? Has the book been written to speak clearly to these readers?

3. Focus. If the book is a novel, does it depict the life or lives of one or two or three main characters, and not more? If the book is nonfiction, does it have one unifying theme?

4. Completeness. Does the work contain everything it needs?

5. Organization. Are the elements organized in the best possible order?

6. Relevance. Are there some parts that should be completely cut?

7. Expansion. Are there some parts of the work that need more details?

8. Reduction. Are there some parts of the work that need to be made shorter?

9. Transitions. Are there enough transitional passages, and are they clear?

10. Effectiveness. Does the work accomplish its specific central purpose? Does the work accomplish the general purpose of writing: to inform, to entertain, to enlighten?

What do Copyeditors do?

Copy editors work on specific problems in these ten areas:

1. Are there any spelling or typographical errors?

2. Are there errors in grammar and punctuation?

3. Are there mistakes in meaning and usage?

4. Is the work uniformly consistent with the house style for grammar and other formatting?

5. If the work is an electronic publication (ebook, email, or web page) do all the hyperlinks work? Are there any other glitches, such as files that do not open, or HTML tags that are miscoded?

6. If the work is an electronic publication, has it been designed to meet WAI and Section 508 accessibility standards?

7. Are the facts correct?

8. Is the formatting OK: titles and headers in the right place, pages numbered

correctly, and so on?

9. Is the front matter and supplementary material (appendices, bibliography, index) free from mistakes?

10. Can the meaning be made clearer by rewriting awkward sentences and awkward paragraphs? (This is style editing, and often the copyeditor will contact the author and ask the author to improve the murky passages).

The Value of Editing and Revising

Henry Miller, who wrote semi-autobiographical romances, forbid his publishers to change any words in his books. In this respect, Miller is a rare bird. Most writers welcome caring and sensitive editing.

A good amount of editing is dedicated to cutting things out. As Mark Twain explained:
"Writing is easy. All you have to do is cross out the wrong words."

Editing works its wonders in countless ways. In the dangling participle below, the poor President is stretched too thin.
"Stretching for the miles, the President watched the stars in the night sky."

Since the 1960s, the publishing industry has changed. Large companies gobble up the smaller ones. Money is the bottom line; and the work of editing, is one of the first things to be deleted. For writers who chase the dream of finding fame with a large publishing house, and for writers who go alone and self-publish their own books, the same Socratic lesson is true: "Edit thyself."

A well-edited manuscript gives the writer a much better chance of finding a literary agent or a publisher. A well-edited self-published book silences the critics, and gives the author a fighting chance for success.

15
Eleven Deadly Sins of Literary Style

by Michael Pastore

In one of his *Notebooks,* Samuel Butler notes that a rough draft of one of Plato's *Dialogues* had been discovered, and the first paragraph 'was written in seventy different forms.' ... Butler wrote:

"A man may, and ought to take a great deal of pains to write clearly, tersely and euphemistically: he will write many a sentence three or four times over — to do much more than this is worse than not rewriting at all: he will be at great pains to see that he does not repeat himself, to arrange his matter in the way that shall best enable the reader to master it, to cut out superfluous words and, even more, to eschew irrelevant matter: but in each case he will be thinking not of his own style but of his reader's convenience."

Butler believed in rewriting, but not too much. In his semi-autobiographical novel *The Way of All Flesh* (1903), the protagonist commits a number of foolish transgressions, but the author never lapses into any of the seven classic sins of style: verbosity, flabbiness, circumlocution, stodginess, abstractions, cliches, and monotony of rhythm. Here below are eleven blunders to avoid in the first draft, or to remove in the second.

1. The meaning is not clear.

Said Matthew Arnold: "People think that I can teach them style. What stuff it is. Have something to say and say it as clearly as you can. That is the only secret of style."

2. There are too many words which are needless, redundant, excessive, unnecessary, circumlocutious, plethoric, and superfluous.

William Strunk, Jr. wrote: "Omit needless words. Vigorous writing is concise. A sentence should contain no unnecessary words, a paragraph no unnecessary sentences, for the same reason that a drawing should have no unnecessary lines and a machine no unnecessary parts."

3. Purple is thy prose.

Horace invented the expression: *"purpureus pannus"* (purple patch) for a passage too splendiferous and ornate. Colette wrote: "Drop the literature!"

4. The prose is ordinary, otherwise known as "grey prose".

The antidote is prescribed by Brenda Ueland: "Whenever a sentence came from the true self, and it was felt — it was alive. Be bold. Be free. Be truthful."
    Sometimes the sounds of the sentences are spoiled by dissonance. In these cases, the writer can improve his euphony, by listening to the rhythm of his sentences, and varying their length.

5. The work rains cliches and snows weak metaphors.

Schopenhauer writes, in an essay, *On Thinking for Oneself:* "The characteristic sign of a mind of the highest order is that it always judges at first hand. Everything it advances is the result of thinking for itself; and this is everywhere evident by the way in which it gives its thoughts utterance."

6. The work lacks dramatic quality, or arouses no interest in the reader.

Quentin Crisp crisply explains how to be interesting: "No one is boring who will tell the truth about himself."

7. The writing is abstract and filled with generalizations.

"An abstract style is always bad," writes Alain. "Your sentences should be full of stones, metals, chairs, tables, animals, men and women."

8. The sentence contains the approximate word, instead of the precise word.

Mark Twain always looked for the very best. "The difference between the right and the nearly right word is the same as that between lightning and the lightning bug."

9. The writing is not appropriate for the intended audience.

Know your audience before your speak or write. Are you using terms or names that might be unfamiliar to your readers? Do not send them scrambling to the enclycopedia: provide your reader with all the information necessary to fully understand your work.

10. The writing is insincere.

Hear George Orwell, is his indispensable essay, *Politics and the English Language:*
   "The great enemy of clear language is insincerity. When there is a gap between one's real and one's declared aims, one turns, as it were instinctively, to long words and exhausted idioms, like a cuttlefish squirting out ink."
   The power of sincerity is sincerely expressed by Emerson:
   "The way to speak and write what shall not go out of fashion is to speak and write sincerely. The argument which has not the power to reach my own practice, I may well doubt will fail to reach yours. But take Sidney's maxim: 'Look in thy heart and write.' He that writes to himself writes to an eternal public. That statement only is fit to be made public which you have come at in an attempting to satisfy your own spiritual curiosity."

11. The writer values style above substance.

The 16th-century Italian poet, Pier Angelo Manzolli — known as Palingenius — wrote:
   Their words were glittering ornaments, but lacked inner meaning.
   (Verba nitent phaleris, at nullas verba medullas, Intus habent.)

   When your words merely fizz and sparkle like champagne on a shallow plate — follow Friedrich Nietzsche's sage advice: "To improve your style means to improve your ideas, nothing else."

16
Maxwell Perkins
Teaches Editing and Writing

by Michael Pastore

"Artists, Saints ... are on the frontiers of time —
pioneers and guides to the future."
— Maxwell Perkins, letter, May 31, 1944

Book publishing in the USA once flourished in a golden age, and Maxwell Perkins was its Pericles. As an editor at Charles Scribner's Sons for 37 years, Perkins shaped the lives and works of America's best-known writers. Who were the writers? Ernest Hemingway, Thomas Wolfe, F. Scott Fitzgerald, Nancy Hale, Sherwood Anderson, Ring Lardner, Erskine Caldwell, John Hall Wheelock, John P. Marquand, Marjorie Kinnan Rawlings, Taylor Caldwell, James Jones, Marcia Davenport, William Lyon Phelps, and Allen Tate. For these writers and others, Perkins played the role of friend, adviser, psychiatrist, banker and lending institution, executor, and even — during the legendary wrestling bout between Hemingway and Max Eastman — guidance counselor and referee.

First and last, Maxwell Evarts Perkins (1884–1947) was an extraordinary editor. Perkins's editing skills are legendary, but less known is the quintessence of his technique. Underlying his many-faceted method, Perkins possessed a gift for conversation, for listening to meanings and ambience beneath the humble and not-so-humble words. To a writer he once wrote that he would be frightened every time he met a charming young woman. That brave degree of self-revelation evoked respect, honesty and depth from colleagues, authors, and friends.

Seeing and listening — with passionate attention — is the foundation of all good writing and editing. Creation's next phase consists in understanding, and then expressing, precisely what we see and hear. The following twenty ideas epitomize Perkins's essential wisdom about writing, editing, publishing, and literary technique.

1. Trust Yourself.

In a 1921 letter to F. Scott Fitzgerald, Perkins wrote: "Do not ever defer to my judgment — for a writer of any account should speak for himself."
The work of the editor is to find problems and make suggestions; the writer should make the key decisions, and must always write what she feels, wants, and believes.

2. Write From Your Own Experience.

Perkins often said that one's own self and life form the essence of all great fiction. As examples he cited the autobiographical novels *David Copperfield* by Dickens, *Pendennis* by Thackeray, *The Genius* by Dreiser, and Tolstoy's *War and Peace.*

3. Write Not For Money, Write What is Original and Sincere.

Books are more than mere amusements: books matter. Perkins cited the words of Ford Maddox Ford, who wrote to him in 1937 and lamented that modern publishing "has become a racket, a mad pursuit of the bestseller." Perkins agreed, and said that that situation had been dominant for the past six years.
   Contemporary books about how to write "books that sell" — and how to find a publisher for these books — advise writers to follow a formula, and to imitate the canned fiction that sells. Perkins disagreed. He insisted that writers should never write what is popular and commonplace. Authors should write their own novels: whatever is rare, sincere, unique.

4. Focus Your Fierce Wrath.

In a letter to an unidentified author, Perkins tells the writer to be careful with her/his *saeva indignatio* — fierce wrath. This Latin phrase first appeared in Virgil's *Aeneid,* and was adapted and expanded by Jonathan Swift for his epitaph. Swift used the phrase to emphasize his anger at humanity's injustices, follies, incompetence, ignorance, and fatal mistakes. Today, the term *saeva indignatio* refers to the anger of dedicated artists and fighters for social justice.

Perkins never tells his unknown author to damp his fiery passion. He cautions the writer to be objective — not spiteful — when writing about sensitive issues. "If you make your reader mad," writes Perkins, "it does not make any difference how cogent is your reasoning."

5. Rewrite From Your Reader's Point of View.

Perkins would have endorsed Aristotle's maxim: "Think like a philosopher, speak like a common man." He urges his writers to revise based on the question, "How would this passage sound to a typical reader?" In this way he helped writers to build a bridge between the often-conflicting shores of the need to be unique, and the need to communicate clearly.

6. Read the Best Books — Again and Again.

The great books of the world are the writers' university. Perkins frequently cited them as he explained to writers how to improve specific parts of their novels. Perkins advised writers to read *Anna Karenina,* and *War and Peace* — especially the latter — every year. It has been noted that Perkins sought to find and cultivate an American author and novel that could capture the multifarious energies and spirit of America in the same way that Tolstoy illuminated the Russian heart and nation in *War and Peace.*

7. Oppose Censorship and Support Freedom of Expression.

In his letters, Perkins often writes replies to angry readers who are offended by passages in books published by Scribners. Perkins cites Plato's endorsement of censorship, and suppression of poetry and music, stating that Plato believed that a nation would be happier "if it were not disturbed by new ideas, or by revelations of reality." Perkins wrote that although this is a position worth considering, the duty of a publisher is to publish a variety of opinions. It is useful to show vice in literature, because in this way, people will see it for what it is, and thereby learn that it is something to be avoided. "We're not a nation of children," Perkins writes. Adults are — theoretically at least — capable of evaluating what they read.

8. Learn to perceive life and books directly.

Perkins advises authors to get their education by "seeing, hearing, and reading." He cautions the author about the dangers of formal education, which forms the habit of looking at life through a lens of literature of the past — instead of Zen-like, directly, with one's own ideas and eyes. If we see for ourselves, then we can write about the hungry child on our own street corner, not the hungry child personified by, say, Oliver Twist.

9. Understand the nature and importance of dialogue.

Perkins explains the difference between secondhand material — something told — and firsthand material, something heard and seen. Firsthand material is more powerful. Dialogue is one of the best ways to let characters reveal themselves. Do not explain too much — just let your characters do the talking.

10. Be flexible.

Do not let your own plot constrain you. Be open to change as the novel grows. Writing naturally — like tossing your hat onto a peg without too much thinking about it — is the best way to create something genuine.

11. Take your time.

Perkins — in a very kind rejection letter — explains to the writer that the book has failed because it has been rushed. Novels are so difficult to write because they take a long time, and the best writers are besieged by doubt, anxiety, despair. The characters in the novel must become intimately integrated with the background and events. All things must fit precisely, not — in the metaphor by Schopenhauer — like a glove on the hand, but like the hand's skin. To achieve this unity the writer needs to ponder his/her characters and scenes for a long time.

12. Organize your ideas by themes.

Vladimir Nabokov confessed that all his novels were written on small cards, which would be constantly shuffled and rearranged. Perkins advises writers to write down ideas in notebooks, and then organize these pages by keywords on specific themes. After a while, the writer will possess "an immense fund to draw on". (Today, of course, organizing ideas with paper and cards is cumbersome compared with the magic of organizing with computers and the right software. Despite the change in technology, the same concept applies.) Perkins admits that although he believed in this system wholeheartedly, he never practiced it himself.

13. Value vitality and intensity.

F. Scott Fitzgerald's first book, *This Side of Paradise,* was published in 1920. Perkins's acceptance letter to the author praised the book, stating "It abounds in energy and life."

   To another author — of the rejected book — Perkins says that the book would fail to capture the reality, and fail to move the reader. Perkins writes: "This has nothing to do with technique, or structure, or anything of that kind, but only the ability of a writer to feel with intensity himself, and then so express himself as to make the readers feel that way too."

14. Distinguish episodes from incidents.

Episodes need to be developed in great detail, whereas incidents should not be too long or to detailed. Perkins has borrowed this essential idea from Henry Fielding. In his comic novel *Tom Jones,* Fielding writes: "When any extraordinary scene presents itself (as we trust will often be the case), we shall spare no pains nor paper to open it at large to the reader; but if whole years should pass without producing anything worthy of his notice, we shall not be afraid of this and leave such periods of time totally unobserved."

15. Capture the precise feeling of the scene.

Perkins claims that whenever a genuine author writes about a specific day, he can recall — and express — the unique qualities of that day. What was the temperature? The smells in the air? The unique thoughts he was thinking and emotions he was feeling? ... Writers, says Perkins, remember precisely these kinds of things.

16. Do not read about writing while you are writing.

When you are writing a novel, too much thinking about technique leads to distraction and confusion. In *Zorba the Greek,* the novel by Kazantzakis, Zorba tells his boss, the writer, that the boss "thinks too much". Zorba reminds the boss about the centipede, who one day began to watch and wonder about how all his legs can move without entanglements. Baffled by these unnecessary reflections, the poor insect could hardly move at all!

17. To achieve depth and perspective, write about past events, not immediate ones.

Goethe has said that one can see accurately only from great heights. Perkins writes that in journalism we can write quickly and effectively, but not so in writing novels. The novel-writer needs time to unconsciously process and transform events.

18. Let style take care of itself.

Remember Matthew Arnold's famous formula for simplicity and excellence in literary style: "Have something to say and say it is clearly as you can." Perkins, too, believed that style takes care of itself, whenever the author can see the book as a whole.

19. Choose your titles with the utmost care.

Good titles sell books, and keep the novel burning in the readers' minds. Thomas Wolfe wanted to call his first novel 'O Lost'. Working with Perkins, they agreed on the final title: *Look Homeward Angel.*
    One could fill a book with the theme: "Terrible titles changed to good ones." When Margaret Mitchell wanted to call her Civil War novel, 'Tomorrow is Another Day' — her editor suggested a change to the memorable title — *Gone With The Wind.*

20. Cut the unnecessary: vigorous writing is concise.

Perkins knew the importance of choosing just the right of amount of details. Thomas Wolfe once wrote more than 100,000 words — when all that was needed was a brief introduction. What Wolfe had written was extraordinary, but — Perkins asked — did it have a place in this particular manuscript? ... The editor and author together tackled the painful task of revision. In *The Story Of A Novel* (1936), Wolfe wrote: "My spirit quivered at the bloody execution. My soul recoiled before the courage of so many lovely things cut out upon which my heart was set. But it had to be done, and we did it."

§

The genius of Perkins is reflected in one more gemlike facet: faith. Although calm and clear in his literary judgments, passion fired his mind and soul. Perkins believed passionately in his writers. He believed that the world needed the new books — the genuinely new — as well as the classics of old. And he believed in the value and strength of that multifarious prose form we call "the novel", as the most enjoyable and captivating method for transmitting information, feelings, values, wisdom, and ideas.

§ §

Learn More About Maxwell Perkins

Essential reading for all Perkins's admirers is *Editor to Author: the Letters of Maxwell E. Perkins*. (Edited by John Hall Wheelock. Charles Scribner's Sons, 1950, 1979, 1981). Other excellent works reflecting on Perkins's character and skills include *The Story of a Novel* (by Thomas Wolfe. Charles Scribner's Sons,1936); *Max Perkins, Editor of Genius* (by A. Scott Berg. E. P. Dutton, 1978); and *To Loot My Life Clean: The Thomas Wolfe — Maxwell Perkins Correspondence* (edited by Matthew J. Bruccoli and Park Bucker, University of South Carolina Press, 2000). See also, two essays in the *Saturday Review: Catalyst for Genius* by Struthers Burt; and *Thomas Wolfe Did Not Kill Maxwell Perkins,* by Edward C. Aswell.

17
26 Questions for Editing
and Revising Nonfiction Books

by Michael Pastore

Every good book is unique, and presents us with a fresh vision. A formula cannot be used to write, to revise, or to edit an original book.

This list of questions should not be used as a cookie-cutter, but simply as a guide, for editors and authors, to identify some of the strong and not-so-strong aspects of the nonfiction manuscript. Of the three varieties of manuscript editing — substantive editing, line editing, and copyediting — these 26 questions cover substantive editing only.

A. Subject Matter

1. Uniqueness: Has the author given us some unique ideas; or a fresh perspective on a well-traveled theme?

2. Importance: Is the theme timely, and of interest to many readers?

3. Facts and Opinions: Are the facts correct? ... Are the opinions justified by reasons? ... Are the opinions distinguished from the facts?

4. Target Audience: Has the author clearly defined who the book has been written for? ... Is the content, the style, and the level of complexity appropriate for the book's intended readers?

5. Solutions: Is the writer offering solutions to the problem, or is he merely a voice kvetching in the wilderness?

6. Corroboration: Has the author shown a basic knowledge of what other writers in this field understand about the subject? ... Has the author supported his claims with references from other periodicals and books?

B. Structure

7. Organization (now called: "Information Architecture"): Is the book organized in a manner that effectively conveys the author's central ideas? ... In each chapter, the author must carefully decide the best way to organize the book's ideas: A) chronologically; B) by subject; C) by simple to complex; D) by known to unknown; E) by particular to general (or vice versa); F) by order of climax; or G) by basic enumeration.

8. Rhetorical modes (a.k.a., modes of discourse). For each important idea, has the author examined which of the 4 modes would best express it: Exposition; Description; Narration; or Argumentation ?

9. Completeness: Are there ideas or passages or sub-topics that should have been included, but are absent?

10. Economy: Are there ideas or passages that should be cut?

11. Length: Is the overall length of the book appropriate for the subject matter and target audience?

12. Scope: Are there passages that need to be expanded or reduced in length?

13. Emphasis: Would the work benefit from re-examining the book's underlying outline, in order to use the structure to give focus to the points that deserve the most emphasis?

C. Style

14. Clarity: Is the style simple and direct, so that the meaning of each sentence is clear?

15. Reader's Knowledge: Has the COIK problem (coined by Edgar Dale) been avoided? "Clear Only If Known". issues happen whenever the writer mistakenly assumes that the reader already knows some pertinent facts.

16. Interest: Has the author made his subject interesting? ... Has the author added interest by utilizing the fiction-writer's strategy: "Showing is better than telling?", by providing powerful facts, telling details, and person-focused anecdotes and examples?

17. Author's Voice: Is the personality of the author revealed in a confident and natural voice, a voice that carries the reader along with interest, empathy, and trust?

18. Sincerity: Is the writing sincere? ... Is the author writing about a subject that she knows and loves?

19. Personal experiences: Have personal experiences been included, and integrated effectively in the exposition?

20. Affectation: Has the author avoided the seven literary sins of flabbiness, verbosity, circumlocution, stodginess, abstractions, cliches, and monotony of rhythm?

D. Assorted Aspects

21. Title: Is the book's title dynamic and provocative? Does the title accurately capture the essence of the book? ... Are the individual chapter titles interesting and accurate?

22. Opening Paragraph: Has the opening sentence — and the opening paragraph — been carefully written to draw the reader into the chapter? ... Have the opening paragraphs of each chapter been written with that goal in mind?

23. Ending: Does the ending of the book summarize the author's main points and conclusion?

24. Anthology Organization: Has the author organized the chapters into categories that are logical, and have interesting titles? ... Within each category, have the chapters been organized in an effective order?

25. End Matters. Has the author included a bibliography and an index? ... If applicable, has a section with a glossary of terms been included? ... If applicable, is there a list of contributors and brief biographies of each one?

26. Book Covers. Does the book cover art, and the words on the back cover or inside jacket flap, express the spirit of the book?

18
40 Questions For Planning,
Revising, and Editing Fiction

by Michael Pastore

The following questions can be used by the fiction writer to plan her/his novel before beginning, and also to edit the novel after the first draft has been completed.

A. Characters

1. Does your story revolve around 1 or 2 or 3 major characters, or more than that?

2. Are the characters realistic?

3. Are the characters "round", rather than one-dimensional?

4. Are your main characters mindless automatons with hardly an original idea?

5. Do your characters respond in surprising yet believable ways?

6. At the end of your story, is there some significant change in the characters' minds, hearts, or lives?

7. Are these changes believable, or unlikely? Has your story shown the process of the change — or is there little or nothing that would produce such a change?

8. Are your minor characters significant, or could they be cut? Are these minor characters more than one-dimensional? Do the minor characters appear too often and talk too much?

B. Plot, Structure, and Making Scenes

9. Does each one of your characters have a strong purpose? Is this purpose interdependent with the story's plot?

10. Do your characters have a conflict with: other characters? forces in nature? powerful events? or their own selves?

11. Is the conflict balanced? In other words, are the obstacles too simple for the character to conquer, or too overwhelming for the characters to even hope to survive?

12. As the story progresses, does the conflict increase in intensity?

13. Is the plot clear, or impossible to follow?

14. Have you avoided the "soap-opera syndrome"? Do accidents occur at the beginning of your story, or does random trouble strike your characters in the middle or at the end?

15. Is the story interesting? Will the reader be able to guess what happens next? Will the reader care about the fate of your characters?

16. Does the story move along too slowly or too quickly? Does it seem as if the author should have made two books out of one? Or that he/she stretched out one thin tale to fill up an entire book?

C. Dialogue

17. Does the dialogue ring true and natural? Or does it sound forced and contrived?

18. Does the dialogue reveal character or advance the action, or is it ceaseless chitchat and soap-opera trivia about daily events?

19. Would the character speaking know what the character knows? Would she or he use the diction that she or he uses?

20. Are you using "she said" or "he said" after your characters talk, or using less accurate tags such a "she explained", or "he grimaced"?

21. Are you using adverbs in your speech tags — such as "he said sternly" — instead of creating the mood by the character's words and actions?

22. Are the conversations too long, like the dronings in Henry James? Or are they too short, like the primitive grunts in novels by Hemingway?

D. Descriptions, Settings, and Atmosphere

23. Have you clearly depicted the scene before each chapter or change-of-scene within the chapter?

24. Have you described characters and scenes so clearly that a reader who has never seen the character or scene could picture them vividly in her/his mind?

25. Have you divided your descriptive passages into short chunks, and interspersed them efficiently?

26. Have you seen your characters and scenes with fresh eyes, and then communicated this unique seeing?

E. Ideas

27. Does your story contain any profound and controversial ideas, or is it mere entertainment?

28. Have your ideas been embodied in the characters? Or do your characters make long speeches that are disconnected from their lives?

29. Are the ideas presented to show many sides of the issue? Or is the book mere propaganda for a conservative cause?

30. Are your ideas canned, or your own original thoughts?

F. Style, Language, and Technique

31. Have you selected the best narrative point-of-view for your story?

32. If you're using the first-person point-of-view, is the book's main protagonist someone other than the narrator?

33. Are you showing the reader with scenes and with your characters' own words? Or are you simply — too simply — telling the reader about your characters, secondhand?

34. Have you used language originally? Or without any creative flair?

35. Is everything that is meant to be clear, clear?

36. Hast thou avoided the dreaded disease called purple prose, and the pomposity of elevated speech?

37. Have you followed Aristotle's advice: "Think like a philosopher, speak like the common man," ?

38. Have you written from your own experience?

39. Have you trusted your own judgment about your work? Have you written a book that you love and believe in?

40. Have you revised and rewritten your work, again and again and again?

19
The Rejection Slip Rejection Slip

by Michael Pastore

You know how bad the book biz goes
When writers in dejection quip
That editors make them enclose
A self-addressed rejection slip.

—MP

Self-respecting Writers: Are you tired of waiting and waiting and waiting for those humiliating rejection slips from know-nothing publishers? Fight back! Reject their rejections slips!

Six months after your rejection slip arrives, return it to the editor with this brutally impersonal, badly photocopied, form-letter reply. Simply print the page that follows, and then circle the numbers of some or all of the appropriate replies.

Dear Editor:

1. We no longer accept unsolicited rejection slips.

2. Due to the tremendous volume of rejection slips that we receive, we regret that we cannot acknowledge each one with a personal reply.

3. We only consider rejection slips that have been submitted by literary agents.

4. Your rejection slip is not suited to our present needs.

5. Rejection slips must be submitted on clean, 8.5" x 11" paper, printed with a new laser-printer cartridge, and signed by a human hand. Please study the enclosed "Guidelines for Submitting Rejection Slips".

6. Your rejection slip is unpublishable. This is only a personal opinion — other authors may disagree.

7. Your rejection slip never reached us. It is advisable never to send original copies of rejection slips through the mails.

8. Please resubmit your rejeckshun slop after removing grammer and spelling misteaks.

9. Though brief, your rejection slip exudes verbosity, stodginess, circumlocution, vagueness, abstractness, and lack of dramatic quality.

10. Please study our manuscript before submitting future rejection slips.

11. The author no longer works at this house. We are returning your rejection slip herewith.

12. In the future, if you would like your rejection slip returned, kindly include a S.A.S.E.

13. Good luck in placing your rejection slip elsewhere!

The Author

20
On Jargon

by Sir Arthur Quiller-Couch

We parted, Gentlemen, upon a promise to discuss the capital difficulty of Prose, as we have discussed the capital difficulty of Verse. But, although we shall come to it, on second thoughts I ask leave to break the order of my argument and to interpose some words upon a kind of writing which, from a superficial likeness, commonly passes for prose in these days, and by lazy folk is commonly written for prose, yet actually is not prose at all; my excuse being the simple practical one that, by first clearing this sham prose out of the way, we shall the better deal with honest prose when we come to it. The proper difficulties of prose will remain: but we shall be agreed in understanding what it is, or at any rate what it is not, that we talk about. ... I take leave to introduce to you as prose which is not prose and under its real name of Jargon.

You must not confuse this Jargon with what is called Journalese. The two overlap, indeed, and have a knack of assimilating each other's vices. But Jargon finds, maybe, the most of its votaries among good douce people who have never written to or for a newspaper in their life, who would never talk of 'adverse climatic conditions' when they mean 'bad weather'; who have never trifled with verbs such as 'obsess,' 'recrudesce,' 'envisage,' 'adumbrate,' or with phrases such as 'the psychological moment,' 'the true inwardness,' 'it gives furiously to think.' It dallies with Latinity—'sub silentio,' 'de die in diem,' 'cui bono?' (always in the sense, unsuspected by Cicero, of 'What is the profit?')—but not for the sake of style. Your journalist at the worst is an artist in his way: he daubs paint of this kind upon the lily with a professional zeal; the more flagrant (or, to use his own word, arresting) the pigment, the happier is his soul. Like the Babu he is trying all the while to embellish our poor language, to make it more floriferous, more poetical—like the Babu for example who, reporting his mother's death, wrote, 'Regret to inform you, the hand that rocked the cradle has kicked the bucket.'

There is metaphor: *there* is ornament: *there* is a sense of poetry, though as yet groping in a world unrealised. No such gusto marks—no such zeal, artistic or professional, animates—the practitioners of Jargon, who are, most of them (I repeat), douce respectable persons. Caution is its father: the instinct to save everything and especially trouble: its mother, Indolence. It looks precise, but it is not. It is, in these times, *safe:* a thousand men have said it before and not one to your knowledge had been prosecuted for it. And so, like respectability in Chicago, Jargon stalks unchecked in our midst. It is becoming the language of Parliament: it has become the medium through which Boards of Government, County Councils, Syndicates, Committees, Commercial Firms, express the processes as well as the conclusions of their thought and so voice the reason of their being.

Has a Minister to say 'No' in the House of Commons? Some men are constitutionally incapable of saying no: but the Minister conveys it thus— 'The answer to the question is in the negative.' That means 'no.'

Can you discover it to mean anything less, or anything more except that the speaker is a pompous person?—which was no part of the information demanded.

That is Jargon, and it happens to be accurate. But as a rule Jargon is by no means accurate, its method being to walk circumspectly around its target; and its faith, that having done so it has either hit the bull's-eye or at least achieved something equivalent, and safer.

Thus the Clerk of a Board of Guardians will minute that—

> In the case of John Jenkins deceased the coffin provided was of the usual character.

Now this is not accurate. 'In the case of John Jenkins deceased,' for whom a coffin was supplied, it is wholly superfluous to tell us that he is deceased. But actually John Jenkins never had more than one case, and that was the coffin. The Clerk says he had two,—a coffin in a case: but I suspect the Clerk to be mistaken, and I am sure he errs in telling us that the coffin was of the usual character: for coffins have no character, usual or unusual.

For another example (I shall not tell you whence derived)—

> In the case of every candidate who is placed in the first class [So you see the lucky fellow gets a case as well as a first-class. He might be a stuffed animal: perhaps he is] In the case of every candidate who is   placed in the first class the class-list will show by some convenient mark (1) the Section or Sections for proficiency in which he is placed in the first class and (2) the Section or Sections (if any) in which he has passed with special distinction.

'The Section or Sections (if any)'—But, how, if they are not any, could they be indicated by a mark however convenient?

The Examiners will have regard to the style and method of the candidate's answers, and will give credit for excellence *in these respects*.

Have you begun to detect the two main vices of Jargon? The first is that it uses circumlocution rather than short straight speech. It says 'In the case of John Jenkins deceased, the coffin' when it means 'John Jenkins's coffin': and its yea is not yea, neither is its nay nay: but its answer is in the affirmative or in the negative, as the foolish and superfluous 'case' may be. The second vice is that it habitually chooses vague woolly abstract nouns rather than concrete ones. I shall have something to say by-and-by about the concrete noun, and how you should ever be struggling for it whether in prose or in verse. For the moment I content myself with advising you, if you would write masculine English, never to forget the old tag of your Latin Grammar—

> Masculine will only be
> Things that you can touch and see.

But since these lectures are meant to be a course in First Aid to writing, I will content myself with one or two extremely rough rules: yet I shall be disappointed if you do not find them serviceable.

The first is:—Whenever in your reading you come across one of these words, *case, instance, character, nature, condition, persuasion, degree*— whenever in writing your pen betrays you to one or another of them—pull yourself up and take thought. If it be 'case' (I choose it as Jargon's dearest child—'in Heaven yclept Metonomy') turn to the dictionary, if you will, and seek out what meaning can be derived from *casus*, its Latin ancestor: then try how, with a little trouble, you can extricate yourself from that case. The odds are, you will feel like a butterfly who has discarded his chrysalis.

Here are some specimens to try your hand on–

> (1) All those tears which inundated Lord Hugh Cecil's head were dry in the case of Mr Harold Cox.

Poor Mr Cox! left gasping in his aquarium!

> (2) [From a cigar-merchant] In any case, let us send you a case on approval.

> (3) It is contended that Consols have fallen in consequence: but such is by no means the case.

'Such,' by the way, is another spoilt child of Jargon, especially in

Committee's Rules—'Co-opted members may be eligible as such; such members to continue to serve for such time as'—and so on.

> (4) Even in the purely Celtic areas, only in two or three cases do the Bishops bear Celtic names.

For 'cases' read 'dioceses.'

> *Instance.* In most instances the players were below their form.

But what were they playing at? Instances?

> *Character—Nature.* There can be no doubt that the accident was caused through the dangerous nature of the spot, the hidden character of the by-road, and the utter absence of any warning or danger signal.

Mark the foggy wording of it all! And yet the man hit something and broke his neck! Contrast that explanation with the verdict of a coroner's jury in the West of England on a drowned postman—'We find that deceased met his death by an act of God, caused by sudden overflowing of the river Walkhan and helped out by the scandalous neglect of the way-wardens.'

> The Aintree course is notoriously of a trying nature.
> On account of its light character, purity and age, Usher's whiskey is a whiskey that will agree with you.

Order. The mésalliance was of a pronounced order.

> *Condition.* He was conveyed to his place of residence in an intoxicated condition.

'He was carried home drunk.'

> *Quality and Section.* Mr —, exhibiting no less than five works, all of a superior quality, figures prominently in the oil section.

This was written of an exhibition of pictures.

> *Degree.* A singular degree of rarity prevails in the earlier editions of this romance.

That is Jargon. In prose it runs simply 'The earlier editions of this romance are rare'—or 'are very rare'—or even (if you believe what I take leave to doubt), 'are singularly rare'; which should mean that they are rarer than the editions of any other work in the world.

Now what I ask you to consider about these quotations is that in each the writer was using Jargon to shirk prose, palming off periphrases upon us when with a little trouble he could have gone straight to the point. 'A singular degree of rarity prevails,' 'the accident was caused through the dangerous nature of the spot,' 'but such is by no means the case.' We may not be capable of much; but we can all write better than that, if we take a little trouble. In place of, 'the Aintree course is of a trying nature' we can surely say 'Aintree is a trying course' or 'the Aintree course is a trying one'—just that and nothing more.

Next, having trained yourself to keep a look-out for these worst offenders (and you will be surprised to find how quickly you get into the way of it), proceed to push your suspicions out among the whole cloudy host of abstract terms. 'How excellent a thing is sleep,' sighed Sancho Panza; 'it wraps a man round like a cloak'—an excellent example, by the way, of how to say a thing concretely: a Jargoneer would have said that 'among the beneficent qualities of sleep its capacity for withdrawing the human consciousness from the contemplation of immediate circumstances may perhaps be accounted not the least remarkable.' How vile a thing—shall we say?—is the abstract noun! It wraps a man's thoughts round like cotton wool.

Here is a pretty little nest of specimens, found in "The Times" newspaper by Messrs. H. W. and F. G. Fowler, authors of that capital little book "The King's English":—

> One of the most important reforms mentioned in the rescript is the unification of the organisation of judicial institutions and the guarantee for all the tribunals of the independence necessary for securing to all classes of the community equality before the law.

I do not dwell on the cacophony; but, to convey a straightforward piece of news, might not the Editor of "The Times" as well employ a man to write:—

One of the most important reforms is that of the Courts, which need a uniform system and to be made independent. In this way only can men be assured that all are equal before the law.

I think he might.

A day or two ago the musical critic of the "Standard" wrote this:—

MR LAMOND IN BEETHOVEN
Mr Frederick Lamond, the Scottish pianist, as an interpreter of Beethoven
has few rivals. At his second recital of the composer's works at Bechstein
Hall on Saturday afternoon he again displayed a complete sympathy and
understanding of his material that extracted the very essence of aesthetic
and musical value from each selection he undertook. The delightful
intimacy of his playing and his unusual force of individual expression
are invaluable assets, which, allied to his technical brilliancy, enable
him to achieve an artistic triumph. The two lengthy Variations in E flat
major (Op. 35) and in D major, the latter on the Turkish March from
'The Ruins of Athens,' when included in the same programme, require
a master hand to provide continuity of interest. *To say that Mr Lamond*
successfully avoided moments that might at times, in these works, have
inclined to comparative disinterestedness, would be but a moderate way
of expressing the remarkable fascination with which his versatile playing
endowed them, but *at the same time* two of the sonatas given included
a similar form of composition, and no matter how intellectually brilliant
may be the interpretation, the extravagant use of a certain mode is bound
in time to become somewhat ineffective. In the Three Sonatas, the E
major (Op. 109), the A major (Op. 2), No. 2, and the C minor (Op. 111),
Mr Lamond signalised his perfect insight into the composer's varying
moods.

Will you not agree with me that here is no writing, here is no prose, here
is not even English, but merely a flux of words to the pen?

Here again is a string, a concatenation—say, rather, a tiara—of gems of
purest ray serene from the dark unfathomed caves of a Scottish newspaper:—

> The Chinese viewpoint, as indicated in this letter, may not be without
> interest to your readers, because it evidently is suggestive of more than
> an academic attempt to explain an unpleasant aspect of things which, if
> allowed to materialise, might suddenly culminate in disaster resembling
> the Chang-Sha riots. It also ventures to illustrate incidents having their
> inception in recent premature endeavours to accelerate the development
> of Protestant missions in China; but we would hope for the sake of
> the interests involved that what my correspondent describes as 'the
> irresponsible ruffian element' may be known by their various religious
> designations only within very restricted areas.

Well, the Chinese have given it up, poor fellows! and are asking the
Christians—as to-day's newspapers inform us—to pray for them. Do you
wonder? But that is, or was, the Chinese 'viewpoint,'—and what a willow-
pattern viewpoint! Observe its delicacy. It does not venture to interest or

be interesting; merely 'to be not without interest.' But it does 'venture to illustrate incidents'—which, for a viewpoint, is brave enough: and this illustration 'is suggestive of something more than an academic attempt to explain an unpleasant aspect of things which, if allowed to materialise, might suddenly culminate.' What materialises? The unpleasant aspect? or the things? Grammar says the 'things,' 'things which if allowed to materialise.' But things are materialised already, and as a condition of their being things. It must be the aspect, then, that materialises. But, if so, it is also the aspect that culminates, and an aspect, however unpleasant, can hardly do that, or at worst cannot culminate in anything resembling the Chang-Sha riots.... I give it up.

Let us turn to another trick of Jargon: the trick of Elegant Variation, so rampant in the Sporting Press that there, without needing to attend these lectures, the Undergraduate detects it for laughter:—

> Hayward and C. B. Fry now faced the bowling; which apparently had no terrors for the Surrey crack. The old Oxonian, however, took some time in settling to work....

Yes, you all recognise it and laugh at it. But why do you practise it in your Essays? An undergraduate brings me an essay on Byron. In an essay on Byron, Byron is (or ought to be) mentioned many times. I expect, nay exact, that Bryon shall be mentioned again and again. But my undergraduate has a blushing sense that to call Byron Byron twice on one page is indelicate. So Byron, after starting bravely as Byron, in the second sentence turns into 'that great but unequal poet' and thenceforward I have as much trouble with Byron as ever Telemachus with Proteus to hold and pin him back to his proper self. Half-way down the page he becomes 'the gloomy master of Newstead': overleaf he is reincarnated into 'the meteoric darling of society': and so proceeds through successive avatars—'this arch-rebel,' 'the author of Childe Harold,' 'the apostle of scorn,' 'the ex-Harrovian, proud, but abnormally sensitive of his club-foot,' 'the martyr of Missolonghi,' 'the pageant-monger of a bleeding heart.' Now this again is Jargon. It does not, as most Jargon does, come of laziness; but it comes of timidity, which is worse. In literature as in life he makes himself felt who not only calls a spade a spade but has the pluck to double spades and re-double.

For another rule—just as rough and ready, but just as useful: Train your suspicions to bristle up whenever you come upon 'as regards,' 'with regard to,' 'in respect of,' 'in connection with,' 'according as to whether,' and the like. They are all dodges of Jargon, circumlocutions for evading this or that simple statement: and I say that it is not enough to avoid them nine times out of ten, or nine-and-ninety times out of a hundred. You should never use them. That is positive enough, I hope? Though I cannot admire his style, I admire the man who wrote to me, 'Re Tennyson—your remarks anent his "In Memoriam" make me sick': for though re is not a preposition of the first water, and 'anent' has enjoyed its day, the finish crowned the work. But here are a few specimens far, very far, worse:–

> The special difficulty in Professor Minocelsi's case [our old friend 'case' again] arose *in connexion with* the view he holds *relative to* the historical value of the opening pages of Genesis.

That is Jargon. In prose, even taking the miserable sentence as it stands constructed, we should write 'the difficulty arose over the views he holds about the historical value,' etc.

From a popular novelist:—

> I was entirely indifferent *as to* the results of the game, caring nothing at all *as to* whether *I had losses or gains*–

Cut out the first 'as' in 'as to,' and the second 'as to' altogether, and the sentence begins to be prose—'I was indifferent to the results of the game, caring nothing whether I had losses or gains.'

But why, like Dogberry, have 'had losses'? Why not simply 'lose.' Let us try again. 'I was entirely indifferent to the results of the game, caring nothing at all whether I won or lost.'

Still the sentence remains absurd: for the second clause but repeats the first without adding one jot. For if you care not at all whether you win or lose, you must be entirely indifferent to the results of the game. So why not say 'I was careless if I won or lost,' and have done with it?

> A man of simple and charming character, he was fitly *associated with* the distinction of the Order of Merit.

I take this gem with some others from a collection made three years ago, by the "Oxford Magazine"; and I hope you admire it as one beyond price. 'He was associated with the distinction of the Order of Merit' means 'he was given the Order of Merit.' If the members of that Order make a society then he was associated with them; but you cannot associate a man with a distinction. The inventor of such fine writing would doubtless have answered Canning's Needy Knife-grinder with:–

> I associate thee with sixpence! I will see thee in another association first!

But let us close our *florilegium* and attempt to illustrate Jargon by the converse method of taking a famous piece of English (say Hamlet's soliloquy) and remoulding a few lines of it in this fashion:—

> To be, or the contrary? Whether the former or the latter be preferable would seem to admit of some difference of opinion; the answer in the present case being of an affirmative or of a negative character according as to whether one elects on the one hand to mentally suffer the disfavour of fortune, albeit in an extreme degree, or on the other to boldly envisage adverse conditions in the prospect of eventually bringing them to a conclusion. The condition of sleep is similar to, if not indistinguishable from, that of death; and with the addition of finality the former might be considered identical with the latter: so that in this connection it might be argued with regard to sleep that, could the addition be effected, a termination would be put to the endurance of a multiplicity of inconveniences, not to mention a number of downright evils incidental to our fallen humanity, and thus a consummation achieved of a most gratifying nature.

That is Jargon: and to write Jargon is to be perpetually shuffling around in the fog and cotton-wool of abstract terms; to be for ever hearkening, like Ibsen's Peer Gynt, to the voice of the Boyg exhorting you to circumvent the difficulty, to beat the air because it is easier than to flesh your sword in the thing. The first virtue, the touchstone of a masculine style, is its use of the active verb and the concrete noun. When you write in the active voice, 'They gave him a silver teapot,' you write as a man. When you write 'He was made the recipient of a silver teapot,' you write jargon. But at the beginning set even higher store on the concrete noun. Somebody—I think it was FitzGerald—once posited the question 'What would have become of Christianity if Jeremy Bentham had had the writing of the Parables?' Without pursuing that dreadful enquiry I ask you to note how carefully the Parables—those exquisite short stories—speak only of 'things which you can touch and see'—'A sower went forth to sow,' 'The kingdom of heaven is like unto leaven, which a woman took,'—and not the Parables only, but the Sermon on the Mount and almost every verse of the Gospel. The Gospel does not, like my young essayist, fear to repeat a word, if the word be good. The Gospel says 'Render unto Caesar the things that are Caesar's'—not 'Render unto Caesar the things that appertain to that potentate.' The Gospel does not say 'Consider the growth of the lilies,' or even 'Consider how the lilies grow.' It says, 'Consider the lilies, how they grow.'

Or take Shakespeare. I wager you that no writer of English so constantly chooses the concrete word, in phrase after phrase forcing you to touch and see. No writer so insistently teaches the general through the particular. He does it even in "Venus and Adonis" (as Professor Wendell, of Harvard, pointed out in a brilliant little monograph on Shakespeare, published some ten years ago). Read any page of "Venus and Adonis" side by side with any page of Marlowe's "Hero and Leander" and you cannot but mark the contrast: in Shakespeare the definite, particular, visualised image, in Marlowe the beautiful generalisation, the abstract term, the thing seen at a literary remove. Take the two openings, both of which start out with the sunrise. Marlowe begins:–

> Now had the Morn espied her lover's steeds:
> Whereat she starts, puts on her purple weeds,
> And, red for anger that he stay'd so long,
> All headlong throws herself the clouds among.

Shakespeare wastes no words on Aurora and her feelings, but gets to his hero and to business without ado:–

> Even as the sun with purple-colour'd face—
> (You have the sun visualised at once),
> Even as the sun with purple-colour'd face
> Had ta'en his last leave of the weeping morn,
> Rose-cheek'd Adonis hied him to the chase;
> Hunting he loved, but love he laugh'd to scorn.

When Shakespeare has to describe a horse, mark how definite he is:–

> Round-hoof'd, short-jointed, fetlocks shag and long,
> Broad breast, full eye, small head and nostril wide,
> High crest, short ears, straight legs and passing strong;
> Thin mane, thick tail, broad buttock, tender hide.

Or again, in a casual simile, how definite:–

> Upon this promise did he raise his chin,
> Like a dive-dipper peering through a wave,
> Which, being look'd on, ducks as quickly in.

Or take, if you will, Marlowe's description of Hero's first meeting

Leander:–

> It lies not in our power to love or hate,
> For will in us is over-ruled by fate...,

and set against it Shakespeare's description of Venus' last meeting with Adonis, as she came on him lying in his blood:–

> Or as a snail whose tender horns being hit
> Shrinks backward in his shelly cave with pain,
> And there, all smother'd up, in shade doth sit,
> Long after fearing to creep forth again;
>   So, at his bloody view–

I do not deny Marlowe's lines (if you will study the whole passage) to be lovely. You may even judge Shakespeare's to be crude by comparison. But you cannot help noting that whereas Marlowe steadily deals in abstract, nebulous terms, Shakespeare constantly uses concrete ones, which later on he learned to pack into verse, such as:–

> Sleep that knits up the ravell'd sleeve of care.

Is it unfair to instance Marlowe, who died young? Then let us take Webster for the comparison; Webster, a man of genius or of something very like it, and commonly praised by the critics for his mastery over definite, detailed, and what I may call *solidified sensation.* Let us take this admired passage from his "Duchess of Malfy":–

Ferdinand. How doth our sister Duchess bear herself
>>> In her imprisonment?

Basola. Nobly: I'll describe her.
>>> She's sad as one long used to 't, and she seems
>>> Rather to welcome the end of misery
>>> Than shun it: a behaviour so noble
>>> As gives a majesty to adversity

(Note the abstract terms.)
>>> You may discern the shape of loveliness
>>> More perfect in her tears than in her smiles;
>>> She will muse for hours together; and her silence

(Here we first come on the concrete: and beautiful it is.)

> Methinks expresseth more than if she spake.

Now set against this the well-known passage from "Twelfth Night" where the Duke asks and Viola answers a question about someone unknown to him and invented by her–a mere phantasm, in short: yet note how much more definite is the language:–

Viola.	My father had a daughter lov'd a man;
	As it might be, perhaps, were I a woman,
	I should your lordship.
Duke.	And what's her history?
Viola.	A blank, my lord. She never told her love,
	But let concealment, like a worm i' the bud,
	Feed on her damask cheek; she pined in thought,
	And with a green and yellow melancholy
	She sat like Patience on a monument
	Smiling at grief. Was not this love indeed?

Observe (apart from the dramatic skill of it) how, when Shakespeare *has* to use the abstract noun 'concealment,' on an instant it turns into a visible worm 'feeding' on the visible rose; how, having to use a second abstract word 'patience,' at once he solidifies it in tangible stone.

Turning to prose, you may easily assure yourselves that men who have written learnedly on the art agree in treating our maxim—to prefer the concrete term to the abstract, the particular to the general, the definite to the vague—as a canon of rhetoric. Whately has much to say on it. The late Mr E. J. Payne, in one of his admirable prefaces to Burke (prefaces too little known and valued, as too often happens to scholarship hidden away in a schoolbook), illustrated the maxim by setting a passage from Burke's speech "On Conciliation with America" alongside a passage of like purport from Lord Brougham's "Inquiry into the Policy of the European Powers." Here is the deadly parallel:–

> BURKE.
> In large bodies the circulation of power must be less vigorous at the extremities. Nature has said it. The Turk cannot govern AEgypt and Arabia and Curdistan as he governs Thrace; nor has he the same dominion in Crimea and Algiers which he has at Brusa and Smyrna. Despotism itself is obliged to truck and huckster. The Sultan gets such obedience as he can. He governs with a loose rein, that he may govern at all; and the

whole of the force and vigour of his authority in his centre is derived from a prudent relaxation in all his borders.

BROUGHAM.
In all the despotisms of the East, it has been observed that the further any part of the empire is removed from the capital, the more do its inhabitants enjoy some sort of rights and privileges: the more inefficacious is the power of the monarch; and the more feeble and easily decayed is the organisation of the government.

You perceive that Brougham has transferred Burke's thought to his own page: but will you not also perceive how pitiably, by dissolving Burke's vivid particulars into smooth generalities, he has enervated its hold on the mind?

'This particularising style,' comments Mr Payne, 'is the essence of Poetry; and in Prose it is impossible not to be struck with the energy it produces. Brougham's passage is excellent in its way: but it pales before the flashing lights of Burke's sentences. The best instances of this energy of style, he adds, are to be found in the classical writers of the seventeenth century. 'When South says, "An Aristotle was but the rubbish of an Adam, and Athens but the rudiments of Paradise," he communicates more effectually the notion of the difference between the intellect of fallen and of unfallen humanity than in all the philosophy of his sermons put together.'

You may agree with me, or you may not, that South in this passage is expounding trash; but you will agree with Mr Payne and me that he uttered it vividly.

Let me quote to you, as a final example of this vivid style of writing, a passage from Dr John Donne far beyond and above anything that ever lay within South's compass:–

The ashes of an Oak in the Chimney are no epitaph of that Oak, to tell me how high or how large that was; it tells me not what flocks it sheltered while it stood, nor what men it hurt when it fell. The dust of great persons' graves is speechless, too; it says nothing, it distinguishes nothing. As soon the dust of a wretch whom thou wouldest not, as of a prince whom thou couldest not look upon will trouble thine eyes if the wind blow it thither; and when a whirle-wind hath blown the dust of the Churchyard into the Church, and the man sweeps out the dust of the Church into the Churchyard, who will undertake to sift those dusts again and to pronounce, This is the Patrician, this is the noble flowre [flour], this the yeomanly, this the Plebeian bran? So is the death of Iesabel (Iesabel was a Queen) expressed. They shall not say *This is Iesabel;* not only not wonder that it is, nor pity that it should be; but they shall not say, they shall not know, *This is Iesabel.*

Carlyle noted of Goethe, 'his emblematic intellect, his never-failing tendency to transform into *shape,* into *life,* the feeling that may dwell in him. Everything has form, has visual excellence: the poet's imagination bodies forth the forms of things unseen, and his pen turns them into shape.'

Perpend this, Gentlemen, and maybe you will not hereafter set it down to my reproach that I wasted an hour of a May morning in a denunciation of Jargon, and in exhorting you upon a technical matter at first sight so trivial as the choice between abstract and definite words.

A lesson about writing your language may go deeper than language; for language (as in a former lecture I tried to preach to you) is your reason, your *logos.* So long as you prefer abstract words, which express other men's summarised concepts of things, to concrete ones which as near as can be reached to things themselves and are the first-hand material for your thoughts, you will remain, at the best, writers at second-hand. If your language be Jargon, your intellect, if not your whole character, will almost certainly correspond. Where your mind should go straight, it will dodge: the difficulties it should approach with a fair front and grip with a firm hand it will be seeking to evade or circumvent. For the Style is the Man, and where a man's treasure is there his heart, and his brain, and his writing, will be also.

21
Mark Twain's Rules For Writing Romantic Fiction

by Mark Twain (Samuel Clemens)

IT SEEMS TO ME that it was far from right for the Professor of English Literature in Yale, the Professor of English Literature in Columbia, and Wilkie Collies to deliver opinions on Cooper's literature without having read some of it. It would have been much more decorous to keep silent and let persons talk who have read Cooper.

Cooper's art has some defects. In one place in *Deerslayer*, and in the restricted space of two-thirds of a page, Cooper has scored 114 offenses against literary art out of a possible 115. It breaks the record.

There are nineteen rules governing literary art in the domain of romantic fiction — some say twenty-two. In *Deerslayer* Cooper{1} violated eighteen of them. These eighteen require:

1. That a tale shall accomplish something and arrive somewhere. But the *Deerslayer* tale accomplishes nothing and arrives in the air.

2. They require that the episodes of a tale shall be necessary parts of the tale, and shall help to develop it. But as the *Deerslayer* tale is not a tale, and accomplishes nothing and arrives nowhere, the episodes have no rightful place in the work, since there was nothing for them to develop.

3. They require that the personages in a tale shall be alive, except in the case of corpses, and that always the reader shall be able to tell the corpses from the others. But this detail has often been overlooked in the *Deerslayer* tale.

4. They require that the personages in a tale, both dead and alive, shall exhibit a sufficient excuse for being there. But this detail also has been overlooked in the *Deerslayer* tale.

5. They require that when the personages of a tale deal in conversation, the talk shall sound like human talk, and be talk such as human beings would be likely to talk in the given circumstances, and have a discoverable meaning, also a discoverable purpose, and a show of relevancy, and remain

in the neighborhood of the subject in hand, and be interesting to the reader, and help out the tale, and stop when the people cannot think of anything more to say. But this requirement has been ignored from the beginning of the *Deerslayer* tale to the end of it.

6. They require that when the author describes the character of a personage in his tale, the conduct and conversation of that personage shall justify said description. But this law gets little or no attention in the *Deerslayer* tale, as Natty Bumppo's case will amply prove.

7. They require that when a personage talks like an illustrated, gilt- edged, tree-calf, hand-tooled, seven-dollar Friendship's Offering in the beginning of a paragraph, he shall not talk like a negro minstrel in the end of it. But this rule is flung down and danced upon in the *Deerslayer* tale.

8. They require that crass stupidities shall not be played upon the reader as "the craft of the woodsman, the delicate art of the forest," by either the author or the people in the tale. But this rule is persistently violated in the *Deerslayer* tale.

9. They require that the personages of a tale shall confine themselves to possibilities and let miracles alone; or, if they venture a miracle, the author must so plausibly set it forth as to make it look possible and reasonable. But these rules are not respected in the *Deerslayer* tale.

10. They require that the author shall make the reader feel a deep interest in the personages of his tale and in their fate; and that he shall make the reader love the good people in the tale and hate the bad ones. But the reader of the *Deerslayer* tale dislikes the good people in it, is indifferent to the others, and wishes they would all get drowned together.

11. They require that the characters in a tale shall be so clearly defined that the reader can tell beforehand what each will do in a given emergency. But in the *Deerslayer* tale this rule is vacated.

In addition to these large rules there are some little ones. These require that the author shall:

12. *Say* what he is proposing to say, not merely come near it.

13. Use the right word, not its second cousin.

14. Eschew surplusage.

15. Not omit necessary details.

16. Avoid slovenliness of form.

17. Use good grammar.

18. Employ a simple and straightforward style.

Even these seven are coldly and persistently violated in the *Deerslayer* tale.

§

I may be mistaken, but it does seem to me that *Deerslayer* is not a work of art in any sense; it does seem to me that it is destitute of every detail that goes to the making of a work of art; in truth, it seems to me that *Deerslayer* is just simply a literary *delirium tremens*.{2}

A work of art? It has no invention; it has no order, system, sequence, or result; it has no lifelikeness, no thrill, no stir, no seeming of reality; its characters are confusedly drawn, and by their acts and words they prove that they are not the sort of people the author claims that they are; its humor is pathetic; its pathos is funny; its conversations are — oh! indescribable; its love-scenes odious; its English a crime against the language.

Counting these out, what is left is Art. I think we must all admit that.

Notes to *Mark Twain's Rules For Writing Romantic Fiction*

{1} *The Deerslayer,* a novel by James Fenimore Cooper (1789–1851), was published in 1841. Natty Bumppo, the main protagonist, was called "Deerslayer" by the Delaware Indians.

{2} *delirium tremens* means, literally, "trembling delirium", and refers to a state of mental confusion caused by alcoholism, characterized by anxiety, trembling, delusions, and hallucinations.

22

George Sand Gives a Literary Lesson to Flaubert

by George Sand

George Sand knew the difference between (what is now called) commercial fiction and literary fiction. Near the end of her life, Sand wrote many letters to her ex-lover and close friend, Gustave Flaubert. She loved the man but disliked his writings, and disagreed completely with the theory of fiction behind them. She believed that he had taken a wrong turn, not only in paying too much attention to form at the expense of content, but in showing a vision of the world which was far too bleak, far too sordid, far too absent of goodness and beauty and hope.

   No book about the art of writing can teach what Sand's letter attempted to convey: substance, personality, passion, vitality, commitment to humanity, courage, optimism, wisdom, insights about the whole realm of who we are and how we live our lives. It is these qualities which make a great book great. Technique is secondary.

George Sand, from a Letter to Gustave Flaubert

"You must have success after the bad luck which has troubled you deeply. I tell you wherein lie the certain conditions for your success. Keep your cult for form; but pay more attention to the substance. Do not take true virtue for a commonplace in literature. Give it its representative, make honest and strong men pass among the fools and the imbeciles that you love to ridicule. Show what is solid at the bottom of these intellectual abortions; in short, abandon the convention of the realist and return to the true reality, which is a mingling of the beautiful and the ugly, the dull and the brilliant, but in which the desire of good finds its place and its occupation all the same."

23
The Airy Substance We Call Style

by Llewelyn Powys

My Dear Mr. [Warner] Taylor:
It is difficult to analyze the airy substance we call style. At its best it seems to escape all definitions. It is as evasive as life. It would be as hard to predict the dancing flight of a flock of finches or the subterranean movements of a single mole, as to explain a great writer s peculiar gift. The reason for this seems to me to lie in the fact that style is the ultimate expression of the author's unique spiritual consciousness. This spiritual consciousness has been arrived at through various influences. Ancestry has bequeathed to it a certain fundamental disposition, environment has thickened this congenital inclination, and the chance temperament of each individual has flashed it into life out of nowhere.

It has been suggested that style consists in saying what has to be said as exactly as possible. This, however, is a different matter altogether. True style has nothing to do with imparting information lucidly. It is not this. It is the scent of the herb, the mist over the blackberry hedge, the soul of the man. It is begotten of the senses, it is the quintessential feeling, the quintessential thought, of those fleet immediate messengers finding unity at last in the person of the being they serve. All the nights that a man has experienced, clouding in so mysteriously over the native earth; all the dawns that he has witnessed with wakeful eyes, have engendered it. The taste of wheaten bread, the taste of milk and wine, has caused it to grow. The sound of church bells heard in a wild place far from village or town has impelled words to dance like children in a May-day procession. The contact of sea waves against the skin, or the grateful warmth of fire against human nakedness can, and should, have an influence on every sentence. The smell of snow, the smell of a hay cock in the sun, nay the smell that rises from the intestines of a rabbit when a man is paunching it with his pocket knife, should prove its periods.

A perfect style is the perfect expression of a man's secret identity. It makes arrogant claims. It demands that the ordinary everyday world should give attention to the wandering goat-cry of a supreme egoism as sensitive as it is tough. It is for this reason that truly great writers are seldom recognized in their lifetime. Commonplace readers invariably appreciate commonplace writers. They prefer books that reflect ideas and methods of thought with which they are already familiar. At all costs the pamphlets they peruse must be partial and platitudinous. They shrink from that terrible spiritual sincerity that burns like fire and prompts a writer to leave his own seal, his own thumb-mark, upon every page he writes.

If I were to be asked by any young person the best way to acquire a style I would tell him to live intensely. The style of a man is the direct result of his passion for life. Learning and scholarship are of small value here. Style is the affirmation of a man's heightened awareness of existence and always grows up from within, from out of the marrow of his bones.

If it were my task to treat of this matter with undergraduates I should draw their attention to certain notable passages of English prose and show them clearly by specific paragraphs, sentences, or even idiosyncratic words, how these men have succeeded in preserving their spirits on parchment for all time. This particular and singular use of the country's language is beyond the scope of the vulgar. It would seem that the innate complexion of a man's mind finds for itself fitting expression. Powerful and original characters write in a powerful and original way, shallow and commonplace characters write in a shallow and commonplace way. Style has to do with the grace, health, and vigour of a man's soul. It is a secret thing dependent upon a natural depth of feeling and no amount of playing the sedulous ape{1} can pass off as authentic what is in truth counterfeit. Just as in the love between a man and a woman true emotion will find convincing expression so it is with writing. Sham feeling makes sham prose and it is easily recognized as such.

My own method is to give no thought whatever to the form of what I am writing. I put down my ideas as they present themselves pell mell to my mind, fanciful, extravagant, sentimental, bawdy, irreverent, irrelevant, they are all equally welcome. In going over my work, however, I am prepared to spend a great deal of care in endeavouring to find the just word or an adequate balance for any particular paragraph. I have noticed that when I am writing at my best I experience a peculiar physical sensation. I first became aware of this peculiarity at school as a boy of twelve when we were given an essay to write on the Pied Piper. I have never been able to think a subject through before writing. I daresay I should do much better if it were my nature to adopt such a method. I consider the greatest difficulty to be overcome by immature, untrained writers is lack of confidence. They are too self-conscious. When once the pen is in the hand it is important to forget about the opinion of others and to write away after your own fashion with careless, proud indifference.

Yours sincerely,

Llewelyn Powys

Note to *The Airy Substance We Call Style* by Llewelyn Powys (MP)

1. Robert Louis Stevenson (in his book "Memories and Portraits") coined the phrase "the sedulous ape." Stevenson explained how he taught himself to write, by studying and imitating the styles of the authors he loved. He wrote:

"All through my boyhood and youth, I was known and pointed out for the pattern of an idler; and yet I was always busy on my own private end, which was to learn to write. I kept always two books in my pocket, one to read, one to write in. As I walked, my mind was busy fitting what I saw with appropriate words; when I sat by the roadside, I would either read, or a pencil and a penny version-book would be in my hand, to note down the features of the scene or commemorate some halting stanzas. Thus I lived with words. And what I thus wrote was for no ulterior use, it was written consciously for practice. It was not so much that I wished to be an author (though I wished that too) as that I had vowed that I would learn to write. That was a proficiency that tempted me; and I practised to acquire it, as men learn to whittle, in a wager with myself. ...

"This was all excellent, no doubt; so were the diaries I sometimes tried to keep, but always and very speedily discarded, finding them a school of posturing and melancholy self-deception. And yet this was not the most efficient part of my training. Good though it was, it only taught me (so far as I have learned them at all) the lower and less intellectual elements of the art, the choice of the essential note and the right word: things that to a happier constitution had perhaps come by nature. And regarded as training, it had one grave defect; for it set me no standard of achievement. So that there was perhaps more profit, as there was certainly more effort, in my secret labours at home. Whenever I read a book or a passage that particularly pleased me, in which a thing was said or an effect rendered with propriety, in which there was either some conspicuous force or some happy distinction in the style, I must sit down at once and set myself to ape that quality. I was unsuccessful, and I knew it; and tried again, and was again unsuccessful and always unsuccessful; but at least in these vain bouts, I got some practice in rhythm, in harmony, in construction and the co-ordination of parts. I have thus played the sedulous ape to Hazlitt, to Lamb, to Wordsworth, to Sir Thomas Browne, to Defoe, to Hawthorne, to Montaigne, to Baudelaire and to Obermann."

24
On Style

by Arthur Schopenhauer
(Translated by T. Bailey Saunders)

Style is the physiognomy of the mind, and a safer index to character than the face. To imitate another man's style is like wearing a mask, which, be it never so fine, is not long in arousing disgust and abhorrence, because it is lifeless; so that even the ugliest living face is better. Hence those who write in Latin and copy the manner of ancient authors, may be said to speak through a mask; the reader, it is true, hears what they say, but he cannot observe their physiognomy too; he cannot see their *style*. With the Latin works of writers who think for themselves, the case is different, and their style is visible; writers, I mean, who have not condescended to any sort of imitation, such as Scotus Erigena, Petrarch, Bacon, Descartes, Spinoza, and many others. An affectation in style is like making grimaces. Further, the language in which a man writes is the physiognomy of the nation to which he belongs; and here there are many hard and fast differences, beginning from the language of the Greeks, down to that of the Caribbean islanders.

To form a provincial estimate of the value of a writer's productions, it is not directly necessary to know the subject on which he has thought, or what it is that he has said about it; that would imply a perusal of all his works. It will be enough, in the main, to know *how* he has thought. This, which means the essential temper or general quality of his mind, may be precisely determined by his style. A man's style shows the *formal* nature of all his thoughts — the formal nature which can never change, be the subject or the character of his thoughts what it may: it is, as it were, the dough out of which all the contents of his mind are kneaded. When Eulenspiegel was asked how long it would take to walk to the next village, he gave the seemingly incongruous answer: *Walk.* He wanted to find out by the man's pace the distance he would cover in a given time. In the same way, when I have read a few pages of an author, I know fairly well how far he can bring me.

Every mediocre writer tries to mask his own natural style, because in his heart he knows the truth of what I am saying. He is thus forced, at the outset, to give up any attempt at being frank or naive — a privilege which is thereby reserved for superior minds, conscious of their own worth, and therefore sure of themselves. What I mean is that these everyday writers are absolutely unable to resolve upon writing just as they think; because they have a notion that, were they to do so, their work might possibly look very childish and simple. For all that, it would not be without its value. If they would only go honestly to work, and say, quite simply, the things they have really thought, and just as they have thought them, these writers would be readable and, within their own proper sphere, even instructive.

But instead of that, they try to make the reader believe that their thoughts have gone much further and deeper than is really the case. They say what they have to say in long sentences that wind about in a forced and unnatural way; they coin new words and write prolix periods which go round and round the thought and wrap it up in a sort of disguise. They tremble between the two separate aims of communicating what they want to say and of concealing it. Their object is to dress it up so that it may look learned or deep, in order to give people the impression that there is very much more in it than for the moment meets the eye. They either jot down their thoughts bit by bit, in short, ambiguous, and paradoxical sentences, which apparently mean much more than they say, — of this kind of writing Schelling's treatises on natural philosophy are a splendid instance; or else they hold forth with a deluge of words and the most intolerable diffusiveness, as though no end of fuss were necessary to make the reader understand the deep meaning of their sentences, whereas it is some quite simple if not actually trivial idea, — examples of which may be found in plenty in the popular works of Fichte, and the philosophical manuals of a hundred other miserable dunces not worth mentioning; or, again, they try to write in some particular style which they have been pleased to take up and think very grand, a style, for example, *par excellence* profound and scientific, where the reader is tormented to death by the narcotic effect of longspun periods without a single idea in them, — such as are furnished in a special measure by those most impudent of all mortals, the Hegelians{1}; or it may be that it is an intellectual style they have striven after, where it seems as though their object were to go crazy altogether; and so on in many other cases. All these endeavors to put off the *nascetur ridiculus mus*{2} — to avoid showing the funny little creature that is born after such mighty throes — often make it difficult to know what it is that they really mean. And then, too, they write down words, nay, even whole sentences, without attaching any meaning to them themselves, but in the hope that someone else will get sense out of them.

And what is at the bottom of all this? Nothing but the untiring effort to sell words for thoughts; a mode of merchandise that is always trying to make fresh openings for itself, and by means of odd expressions, turns of phrase, and combinations of every sort, whether new or used in a new sense, to produce the appearance of intellect in order to make up for the very painfully felt lack of it.

It is amusing to see how writers with this object in view will attempt first one mannerism and then another, as though they were putting on the mask of intellect! This mask may possibly deceive the inexperienced for a while, until it is seen to be a dead thing, with no life in it at all; it is then laughed at and exchanged for another. Such an author will at one moment write in a dithyrambic vein, as though he were tipsy; at another, nay, on the very next page, he will be pompous, severe, profoundly learned and prolix, stumbling on in the most cumbrous way and chopping up everything very small; like the late Christian Wolf, only in a modern dress. Longest of all lasts the mask of unintelligibility; but this is only in Germany, whither it was introduced by Fichte, perfected by Schelling, and carried to its highest pitch in Hegel — always with the best results.

And yet nothing is easier than to write so that no one can understand; just as contrarily, nothing is more difficult than to express deep things in such a way that every one must necessarily grasp them. All the arts and tricks I have been mentioning are rendered superfluous if the author really has any brains; for that allows him to show himself as he is, and confirms to all time Horace's maxim that good sense is the source and origin of good style:

Scribendi recte sapere est et principium et fons. {3}

But those authors I have named are like certain workers in metal, who try a hundred different compounds to take the place of gold — the only metal which can never have any substitute. Rather than do that, there is nothing against which a writer should be more upon his guard than the manifest endeavor to exhibit more intellect than he really has; because this makes the reader suspect that he possesses very little; since it is always the case that if a man affects anything, whatever it may be, it is just there that he is deficient.

That is why it is praise to an author to say that he is *naive;* it means that he need not shrink from showing himself as he is. Generally speaking, to be *naive* is to be attractive; while lack of naturalness is everywhere repulsive. As a matter of fact we find that every really great writer tries to express his thoughts as purely, clearly, definitely and shortly as possible. Simplicity has always been held to be a mark of truth; it is also a mark of genius. Style receives its beauty from the thought it expresses; but with sham-thinkers the thoughts are supposed to be fine because of the style. Style is nothing but the mere silhouette of thought; and an obscure or bad style means a dull or confused brain.

The first rule, then, for a good style is that *the author should have something to say;* nay, this is in itself almost all that is necessary. Ah, how much it means! The neglect of this rule is a fundamental trait in the philosophical writing, and, in fact, in all the reflective literature, of my country, more especially since Fichte. These writers all let it be seen that they want to appear as though they had something to say; whereas they have nothing to say. Writing of this kind was brought in by the pseudo-philosophers at the Universities, and now it is current everywhere, even among the first literary notabilities of the age. It is the mother of that strained and vague style, where there seem to be two or even more meanings in the sentence; also of that prolix and cumbrous manner of expression, called *le stile empesé* {4}; again, of that mere waste of words which consists in pouring them out like a flood; finally, of that trick of concealing the direst poverty of thought under a farrago of never-ending chatter, which clacks away like a windmill and quite stupefies one — stuff which a man may read for hours together without getting hold of a single clearly expressed and definite idea.{5} However, people are easy-going, and they have formed the habit of reading page upon page of all sorts of such verbiage, without having any particular idea of what the author really means. They fancy it is all as it should be, and fail to discover that he is writing simply for writing's sake.

On the other hand, a good author, fertile in ideas, soon wins his reader's confidence that, when he writes, he has really and truly *something to say;* and this gives the intelligent reader patience to follow him with attention. Such an author, just because he really has something to say, will never fail to express himself in the simplest and most straightforward manner; because his object is to awake the very same thought in the reader that he has in himself, and no other. So he will be able to affirm with Boileau that his thoughts are everywhere open to the light of the day, and that his verse always says something, whether it says it well or ill:

Ma pensée au grand jour partout s'offre et s'expose,
Et mon vers, bien ou mal, dit toujours quelque chose:

while of the writers previously described it may be asserted, in the words of the same poet, that they talk much and never say anything at all — *qui parlant beaucoup ne disent jamais rien.*

Another characteristic of such writers is that they always avoid a positive assertion wherever they can possibly do so, in order to leave a loophole for escape in case of need. Hence they never fail to choose the more *abstract* way of expressing themselves; whereas intelligent people use the more *concrete;* because the latter brings things more within the range of actual demonstration, which is the source of all evidence.

There are many examples proving this preference for abstract expression; and a particularly ridiculous one is afforded by the use of the verb *to condition* in the sense of *to cause* or *to produce*. People say *to condition something* instead of *to cause it,* because being abstract and indefinite it says less; it affirms that *A* cannot happen without *B,* instead of that *A* is caused by *B.* A back door is always left open; and this suits people whose secret knowledge of their own incapacity inspires them with a perpetual terror of all positive assertion; while with other people it is merely the effect of that tendency by which everything that is stupid in literature or bad in life is immediately imitated — a fact proved in either case by the rapid way in which it spreads. The Englishman uses his own judgment in what he writes as well as in what he does; but there is no nation of which this eulogy is less true than of the Germans. The consequence of this state of things is that the word *cause* has of late almost disappeared from the language of literature, and people talk only of *condition.* The fact is worth mentioning because it is so characteristically ridiculous.

The very fact that these commonplace authors are never more than half-conscious when they write, would be enough to account for their dullness of mind and the tedious things they produce. I say they are only half-conscious, because they really do not themselves understand the meaning of the words they use: they take words ready-made and commit them to memory. Hence when they write, it is not so much words as whole phrases that they put together — *phrases banales.* This is the explanation of that palpable lack of clearly-expressed thought in what they say. The fact is that they do not possess the die to give this stamp to their writing; clear thought of their own is just what they have not got. And what do we find in its place? — a vague, enigmatical intermixture of words, current phrases, hackneyed terms, and fashionable expressions. The result is that the foggy stuff they write is like a page printed with very old type.

On the other hand, an intelligent author really speaks to us when he writes, and that is why he is able to rouse our interest and commune with us. It is the intelligent author alone who puts individual words together with a full consciousness of their meaning, and chooses them with deliberate design. Consequently, his discourse stands to that of the writer described above, much as a picture that has been really painted, to one that has been produced by the use of a stencil. In the one case, every word, every touch of the brush, has a special purpose; in the other, all is done mechanically. The same distinction may be observed in music. For just as Lichtenberg says that Garrick's soul seemed to be in every muscle in his body, so it is the omnipresence of intellect that always and everywhere characterizes the work of genius.

I have alluded to the tediousness which marks the works of these writers; and in this connection it is to be observed, generally, that tediousness is of two kinds; objective and subjective. A work is objectively tedious when it contains the defect in question; that is to say, when its author has no perfectly clear thought or knowledge to communicate. For if a man has any clear thought or knowledge in him, his aim will be to communicate it, and he will direct his energies to this end; so that the ideas he furnishes are everywhere clearly expressed. The result is that he is neither diffuse, nor unmeaning, nor confused, and consequently not tedious. In such a case, even though the author is at bottom in error, the error is at any rate clearly worked out and well thought over, so that it is at least formally correct; and thus some value always attaches to the work. But for the same reason a work that is objectively tedious is at all times devoid of any value whatever.

The other kind of tediousness is only relative: a reader may find a work dull because he has no interest in the question treated of in it, and this means that his intellect is restricted. The best work may, therefore, be tedious subjectively, tedious, I mean, to this or that particular person; just as, contrarity, the worst work may be subjectively engrossing to this or that particular person who has an interest in the question treated of, or in the writer of the book.

It would generally serve writers in good stead if they would see that, whilst a man should, if possible, think like a great genius, he should talk the same language as everyone else. Authors should use common words to say uncommon things. But they do just the opposite. We find them trying to wrap up trivial ideas in grand words, and to clothe their very ordinary thoughts in the most extraordinary phrases, the most far-fetched, unnatural, and out-of-the-way expressions. Their sentences perpetually stalk about on stilts. They take so much pleasure in bombast, and write in such a high-flown, bloated, affected, hyperbolical and acrobatic style that their prototype is Ancient Pistol, whom his friend Falstaff once impatiently told to say what he had to say *like a man of this world.* {6}

There is no expression in any other language exactly answering to the French *stile empesé;* but the thing itself exists all the more often. When associated with affectation, it is in literature what assumption of dignity, grand airs and primness are in society; and equally intolerable. Dullness of mind is fond of donning this dress; just as an ordinary life it is stupid people who like being demure and formal.

An author who writes in the prim style resembles a man who dresses himself up in order to avoid being confounded or put on the same level with a mob — a risk never run by the *gentleman,* even in his worst clothes. The plebeian may be known by a certain showiness of attire and a wish to have everything spick and span; and in the same way, the commonplace person is betrayed by his style.

Nevertheless, an author follows a false aim if he tries to write exactly as he speaks. There is no style of writing but should have a certain trace of kinship with the *epigraphic* or *monumental* style, which is, indeed, the ancestor of all styles. For an author to write as he speaks is just as reprehensible as the opposite fault, to speak as he writes; for this gives a pedantic effect to what he says, and at the same time makes him hardly intelligible.

An obscure and vague manner of expression is always and everywhere a very bad sign. In ninety-nine cases out of a hundred it comes from vagueness of thought; and this again almost always means that there is something radically wrong and incongruous about the thought itself — in a word, that it is incorrect. When a right thought springs up in the mind, it strives after expression and is not long in reaching it; for clear thought easily finds words to fit it. If a man is capable of thinking anything at all, he is also always able to express it in clear, intelligible, and unambiguous terms. Those writers who construct difficult, obscure, involved, and equivocal sentences, most certainly do not know aright what it is that they want to say: they have only a dull consciousness of it, which is still in the stage of struggle to shape itself as thought. Often, indeed, their desire is to conceal from themselves and others that they really have nothing at all to say. They wish to appear to know what they do not know, to think what they do not think, to say what they do not say. If a man has some real communication to make, which will he choose — an indistinct or a clear way of expressing himself? Even Quintilian remarks that things which are said by a highly educated man are often easier to understand and much clearer; and that the less educated a man is, the more obscurely he will write — *plerumque accidit ut faciliora sint ad intelligendum et lucidiora multo que a doctissimo quoque dicuntur .... Erit ergo etiam obscurior quo quisque deterior.*

An author should avoid enigmatical phrases; he should know whether he wants to say a thing or does not want to say it. It is this indecision of style that makes so many writers insipid. The only case that offers an exception to this rule arises when it is necessary to make a remark that is in some way improper.

As exaggeration generally produces an effect the opposite of that aimed at; so words, it is true, serve to make thought intelligible — but only up to a certain point. If words are heaped up beyond it, the thought becomes more and more obscure again. To find where the point lies is the problem of style, and the business of the critical faculty; for a word too much always defeats its purpose. This is what Voltaire means when he says that *the adjective is the enemy of the substantive.* But, as we have seen, many people try to conceal their poverty of thought under a flood of verbiage.

Accordingly let all redundancy be avoided, all stringing together of remarks which have no meaning and are not worth perusal. A writer must make a sparing use of the reader's time, patience and attention; so as to lead him to believe that his author writes what is worth careful study, and will reward the time spent upon it. It is always better to omit something good than to add that which is not worth saying at all. This is the right application of Hesiod's maxim — *pleon aemisu pantos* {7} — the half is more than the whole. *Le secret pour être ennuyeux, c'est de tout dire.*{8} Therefore, if possible, the quintessence only! mere leading thoughts! nothing that the reader would think for himself. To use many words to communicate few thoughts is everywhere the unmistakable sign of mediocrity. To gather much thought into few words stamps the man of genius.

Truth is most beautiful undraped; and the impression it makes is deep in proportion as its expression has been simple. This is so, partly because it then takes unobstructed possession of the hearer's whole soul, and leaves him no by-thought to distract him; partly, also, because he feels that here he is not being corrupted or cheated by the arts of rhetoric, but that all the effect of what is said comes from the thing itself. For instance, what declamation on the vanity of human existence could ever be more telling than the words of Job? *Man that is born of a woman hath but a short time to live and is full of misery. He cometh up, and is cut down, like a flower; he fleeth as it were a shadow, and never continueth in one stay.*

For the same reason Goethe's naive poetry is incomparably greater than Schiller's rhetoric. It is this, again, that makes many popular songs so affecting. As in architecture an excess of decoration is to be avoided, so in the art of literature a writer must guard against all rhetorical finery, all useless amplification, and all superfluity of expression in general; in a word, he must strive after *chastity* of style. Every word that can be spared is hurtful if it remains. The law of simplicity and naivete holds good of all fine art; for it is quite possible to be at once simple and sublime.

True brevity of expression consists in everywhere saying only what is worth saying, and in avoiding tedious detail about things which everyone can supply for himself. This involves correct discrimination between what it necessary and what is superfluous. A writer should never be brief at the expense of being clear, to say nothing of being grammatical. It shows lamentable want of judgment to weaken the expression of a thought, or to stunt the meaning of a period for the sake of using a few words less. But this is the precise endeavor of that false brevity nowadays so much in vogue, which proceeds by leaving out useful words and even by sacrificing grammar and logic. It is not only that such writers spare a word by making a single verb or adjective do duty for several different periods, so that the reader, as it were, has to grope his way through them in the dark; they also practice, in many other respects, an unseemingly economy of speech, in the effort to produce what they foolishly take to be brevity of expression and conciseness of style. By omitting something that might have thrown a light over the whole sentence, they turn it into a conundrum, which the reader tries to solve by going over it again and again.{9}

It is wealth and weight of thought, and nothing else, that gives brevity to style, and makes it concise and pregnant. If a writer's ideas are important, luminous, and generally worth communicating, they will necessarily furnish matter and substance enough to fill out the periods which give them expression, and make these in all their parts both grammatically and verbally complete; and so much will this be the case that no one will ever find them hollow, empty or feeble. The diction will everywhere be brief and pregnant, and allow the thought to find intelligible and easy expression, and even unfold and move about with grace.

Therefore instead of contracting his words and forms of speech, let a writer enlarge his thoughts. If a man has been thinned by illness and finds his clothes too big, it is not by cutting them down, but by recovering his usual bodily condition, that he ought to make them fit him again.

Let me here mention an error of style, very prevalent nowadays, and, in the degraded state of literature and the neglect of ancient languages, always on the increase; I mean *subjectivity*. A writer commits this error when he thinks it enough if he himself knows what he means and wants to say, and takes no thought for the reader, who is left to get at the bottom of it as best he can. This is as though the author were holding a monologue; whereas, it ought to be a dialogue; and a dialogue, too, in which he must express himself all the more clearly inasmuch as he cannot hear the questions of his interlocutor.

Style should for this very reason never be subjective, but *objective;* and it will not be objective unless the words are so set down that they directly force the reader to think precisely the same thing as the author thought when he wrote them. Nor will this result be obtained unless the author has always been careful to remember that thought so far follows the law of gravity that it travels from head to paper much more easily than from paper to head; so that he must assist the latter passage by every means in his power. If he does this, a writer's words will have a purely objective effect, like that of a finished picture in oils; whilst the subjective style is not much more certain in its working than spots on the wall, which look like figures only to one whose phantasy has been accidentally aroused by them; other people see nothing but spots and blurs. The difference in question applies to literary method as a whole; but it is often established also in particular instances. For example, in a recently published work I found the following sentence: *I have not written in order to increase the number of existing books.* This means just the opposite of what the writer wanted to say, and is nonsense as well.

He who writes carelessly confesses thereby at the very outset that he does not attach much importance to his own thoughts. For it is only where a man is convinced of the truth and importance of his thoughts, that he feels the enthusiasm necessary for an untiring and assiduous effort to find the clearest, finest, and strongest expression for them, — just as for sacred relics or priceless works of art there are provided silvern or golden receptacles. It was this feeling that led ancient authors, whose thoughts, expressed in their own words, have lived thousands of years, and therefore bear the honored title of *classics,* always to write with care. Plato, indeed, is said to have written the introduction to his *Republic* seventy times over in different ways.{10}

As neglect of dress betrays want of respect for the company a man meets, so a hasty, careless, bad style shows an outrageous lack of regard for the reader, who then rightly punishes it by refusing to read the book. It is especially amusing to see reviewers criticizing the works of others in their own most careless style — the style of a hireling. It is as though a judge were to come into court in dressing-gown and slippers! If I see a man badly and dirtily dressed, I feel some hesitation, at first, in entering into conversation with him: and when, on taking up a book, I am struck at once by the negligence of its style, I put it away.

Good writing should be governed by the rule that a man can think only one thing clearly at a time; and, therefore, that he should not be expected to think two or even more things in one and the same moment. But this is what is done when a writer breaks up his principal sentence into little pieces, for the purpose of pushing into the gaps thus made two or three other thoughts by way of parenthesis; thereby unnecessarily and wantonly confusing the reader. And here it is again my own countrymen who are chiefly in fault. That German lends itself to this way of writing, makes the thing possible, but does not justify it. No prose reads more easily or pleasantly than French, because, as a rule, it is free from the error in question. The Frenchman strings his thoughts together, as far as he can, in the most logical and natural order, and so lays them before his reader one after the other for convenient deliberation, so that every one of them may receive undivided attention. The German, on the other hand, weaves them together into a sentence which he twists and crosses, and crosses and twists again; because he wants to say six things all at once, instead of advancing them one by one. His aim should be to attract and hold the reader's attention; but, above and beyond neglect of this aim, he demands from the reader that he shall set the above mentioned rule at defiance, and think three or four different thoughts at one and the same time; or since that is impossible, that his thoughts shall succeed each other as quickly as the vibrations of a cord. In this way an author lays the foundation of his *stile empesé,* which is then carried to perfection by the use of high-flown, pompous expressions to communicate the simplest things, and other artifices of the same kind.

In those long sentences rich in involved parenthesis, like a box of boxes one within another, and padded out like roast geese stuffed with apples, it is really the *memory* that is chiefly taxed; while it is the understanding and the judgment which should be called into play, instead of having their activity thereby actually hindered and weakened.{11} This kind of sentence furnishes the reader with mere half-phrases, which he is then called upon to collect carefully and store up in his memory, as though they were the pieces of a torn letter, afterwards to be completed and made sense of by the other halves to which they respectively belong. He is expected to go on reading for a little without exercising any thought, nay, exerting only his memory, in the hope that, when he comes to the end of the sentence, he may see its meaning and so receive something to think about; and he is thus given a great deal to learn by heart before obtaining anything to understand. This is manifestly wrong and an abuse of the reader's patience.

The ordinary writer has an unmistakable preference for this style, because it causes the reader to spend time and trouble in understanding that which he would have understood in a moment without it; and this makes it look as though the writer had more depth and intelligence than the reader. This is, indeed, one of those artifices referred to above, by means of which mediocre authors unconsciously, and as it were by instinct, strive to conceal their poverty of thought and give an appearance of the opposite. Their ingenuity in this respect is really astounding.

It is manifestly against all sound reason to put one thought obliquely on top of another, as though both together formed a wooden cross. But this is what is done where a writer interrupts what he has begun to say, for the purpose of inserting some quite alien matter; thus depositing with the reader a meaningless half-sentence, and bidding him keep it until the completion comes. It is much as though a man were to treat his guests by handing them an empty plate, in the hope of something appearing upon it. And commas used for a similar purpose belong to the same family as notes at the foot of the page and parenthesis in the middle of the text; nay, all three differ only in degree. If Demosthenes and Cicero occasionally inserted words by ways of parenthesis, they would have done better to have refrained.

But this style of writing becomes the height of absurdity when the parenthesis are not even fitted into the frame of the sentence, but wedged in so as directly to shatter it. If, for instance, it is an impertinent thing to interrupt another person when he is speaking, it is no less impertinent to interrupt oneself. But all bad, careless, and hasty authors, who scribble with the bread actually before their eyes, use this style of writing six times on a page, and rejoice in it. It consists in — it is advisable to give rule and example together, wherever it is possible — breaking up one phrase in order to glue in another. Nor is it merely out of laziness that they write thus. They do it out of stupidity; they think there is a charming *légèreté* {12} about it; that it gives life to what they say. No doubt there are a few rare cases where such a form of sentence may be pardonable.

Few write in the way in which an architect builds; who, before he sets to work, sketches out his plan, and thinks it over down to its smallest details. Nay, most people write only as though they were playing dominoes; and, as in this game, the pieces are arranged half by design, half by chance, so it is with the sequence and connection of their sentences. They only have an idea of what the general shape of their work will be, and of the aim they set before themselves. Many are ignorant even of this, and write as the coral-insects build; period joins to period, and the Lord only knows what the author means.

Life now-a-days goes at a gallop; and the way in which this affects literature is to make it extremely superficial and slovenly.

Endnotes to *On Style*

AS = Arthur Schopenhauer
TBS = T. Bailey Saunders
MP = Michael Pastore

(1). In their Hegel-gazette, commonly known as *Jahrbücher der wissenschaftlichen Literatur.* (AS)

(2). From Horace, in *Ars Poetcia:* The Latin *"Parturient montes, nascetur ridiculus mus,"* which means in English "The mountains labor and bring forth a ridiculous mouse." (MP)

(3). Horace, in *Ars Poetica:* The Latin is *"Scribendi recte sapere est principium et fons,"* which means in English: "Knowing is the first principle and fountainhead of writing well." (MP)

(4). *le stile empesé* is the style that is formal, starched and stiff. (MP)

(5). Select examples of the art of writing in this style are to be found almost *passim* in the *Jahrbücher* published at Halle, afterwards called the *Deutschen Jahrbücher.* (AS)

(6). *King Henry IV.,* Part II. Act v. Sc. 3. (AS)

(7). From Heisod's work, *Works and Days, 40.* The text is an English transliteration of the Greek words. (MP)

(8). The French *"Le secret pour être ennuyeux, c'est de tout dir,"* means in English: "The secret of being a bore is to tell everything." The remark was written by Voltaire, in his 1737 work, *Discours en vers sur l'homme.* (MP)

(9). In the original, Schopenhauer here enters upon a lengthy examination of certain common errors in the writing and speaking of German. His remarks are addressed to his own countrymen, and would lose all point, even if they were intelligible, in an English translation. But for those who practice their German by conversing or corresponding with Germans, let me recommend what he there says as a useful corrective to a slipshod style, such as can easily be contracted if it is assumed that the natives of a country always know their own language perfectly. (TBS)

(10). It is a fact worth mentioning that the first twelve words of the *Republic* [written by Plato] are placed in the exact order which would be natural in English. (TBS)

(11). This sentence in the original is obviously meant to illustrate the fault of which it speaks. It does so by the use of a construction very common in German, but happily unknown in English; where, however, the fault itself exists none the less, though in different form. (TBS)

(12). The French word *légèreté* means "lightness." (MP)

25
A Perfectly Healthy Sentence

by Henry David Thoreau

A perfectly healthy sentence, it is true, is extremely rare. For the most part we miss the hue and fragrance of the thought; as if we could be satisfied with the dews of the morning or evening without their colors, or the heavens without their azure. The most attractive sentences are, perhaps, not the wisest, but the surest and roundest. They are spoken firmly and conclusively, as if the speaker had a right to know what he says, and if not wise, they have at least been well learned. Sir Walter Raleigh might well be studied if only for the excellence of his style, for he is remarkable in the midst of so many masters. There is a natural emphasis in his style, like a man's tread, and a breathing space between the sentences, which the best of modern writing does not furnish. His chapters are like English parks, or say rather like a Western forest, where the larger growth keeps down the underwood, and one may ride on horseback through the openings. All the distinguished writers of that period possess a greater vigor and naturalness than the more modern,—for it is allowed to slander our own time,—and when we read a quotation from one of them in the midst of a modern author, we seem to have come suddenly upon a greener ground, a greater depth and strength of soil. It is as if a green bough were laid across the page, and we are refreshed as by the sight of fresh grass in midwinter or early spring. You have constantly the warrant of life and experience in what you read. The little that is said is eked out by implication of the much that was done. The sentences are verdurous and blooming as evergreen and flowers, because they are rooted in fact and experience, but our false and florid sentence have only the tints of flowers without their sap or roots. All men are really most attracted by the beauty of plain speech, and they even write in a florid style in imitation of this. They prefer to be misunderstood rather than to come short of its exuberance. Hussein Effendi praised the epistolary style of Ibrahim Pasha to the French traveller Botta, because of "the difficulty of understanding it; there was," he said, "but one person at Jidda, who was capable of understanding and explaining the Pasha's correspondence." A man's whole life is taxed for the least thing well done. It is its net result.

Every sentence is the result of a long probation. Where shall we look for standard English, but to the words of a standard man? The word which is best said came nearest to not being spoken at all, for it is cousin to a deed which the speaker could have better done. Nay, almost it must have taken the place of a deed by some urgent necessity, even by some misfortune, so that the truest writer will be some captive knight, after all. And perhaps the fates had such a design, when, having stored Raleigh so richly with the substance of life and experience, they made him a fast prisoner, and compelled him to make his words his deeds, and transfer to his expression the emphasis and sincerity of his action.

Men have a respect for scholarship and learning greatly out of proportion to the use they commonly serve. We are amused to read how Ben Jonson engaged, that the dull masks with which the royal family and nobility were to be entertained should be "grounded upon antiquity and solid learning." Can there be any greater reproach than an idle learning? Learn to split wood, at least.

The necessity of labor and conversation with many men and things, to the scholar is rarely well remembered; steady labor with the hands, which engrosses the attention also, is unquestionably the best method of removing palaver and sentimentality out of one's style, both of speaking and writing. If he has worked hard from morning till night, though he may have grieved that he could not be watching the train of his thoughts during that time, yet the few hasty lines which at evening record his day's experience will be more musical and true than his freest but idle fancy could have furnished. Surely the writer is to address a world of laborers, and such therefore must be his own discipline. He will not idly dance at his work who has wood to cut and cord before nightfall in the short days of winter; but every stroke will be husbanded, and ring soberly through the wood; and so will the strokes of that scholar's pen, which at evening record the story of the day, ring soberly, yet cheerily, on the ear of the reader, long after the echoes of his axe have died away.

The scholar may be sure that he writes the tougher truth for the calluses on his palms. They give firmness to the sentence. Indeed, the mind never makes a great and successful effort, without a corresponding energy of the body. We are often struck by the force and precision of style to which hard-working men, unpractised in writing, easily attain when required to make the effort. As if plainness, and vigor, and sincerity, the ornaments of style, were better learned on the farm and in the workshop, than in the schools. The sentences written by such rude hands are nervous and tough, like hardened thongs, the sinews of the deer, or the roots of the pine. As for the graces of expression, a great thought is never found in a mean dress; but though it proceed from the lips of the Woloffs, the nine Muses and the three Graces will have conspired to clothe it in fit phrase. Its education has always been liberal, and its implied wit can endow a college. The world, which the Greeks called Beauty, has been made such by being gradually divested of every ornament which was not fitted to endure. The Sibyl, "speaking with inspired mouth, smileless, inornate, and unperfumed, pierces through centuries by the power of the god." The scholar might frequently emulate the propriety and emphasis of the farmer's call to his team, and confess that if that were written it would surpass his labored sentences. Whose are the truly *labored* sentences? From the weak and flimsy periods of the politician and literary man, we are glad to turn even to the description of work, the simple record of the month's labor in the farmer's almanac, to restore our tone and spirits. A sentence should read as if its author, had he held a plough instead of a pen, could have drawn a furrow deep and straight to the end. The scholar requires hard and serious labor to give an impetus to his thought. He will learn to grasp the pen firmly so, and wield it gracefully and effectively, as an axe or a sword. When we consider the weak and nerveless periods of some literary men, who perchance in feet and inches come up to the standard of their race, and are not deficient in girth also, we are amazed at the immense sacrifice of thews and sinews. What! these proportions,–these bones,–and this their work! Hands which could have felled an ox have hewed this fragile matter which would not have tasked a lady's fingers! Can this be a stalwart man's work, who has a marrow in his back and a tendon Achilles in his heel? They who set up the blocks of Stonehenge did somewhat, if they only laid out their strength for once, and stretched themselves.

Yet, after all, the truly efficient laborer will not crowd his day with work, but will saunter to his task surrounded by a wide halo of ease and leisure, and then do but what he loves best. He is anxious only about the fruitful kernels of time. Though the hen should sit all day, she could lay only one egg, and, besides, would not have picked up materials for another. Let a man take time enough for the most trivial deed, though it be but the paring of his nails. The buds swell imperceptibly, without hurry or confusion, as if the short spring days were an eternity.

26
The Life-Work Of A Poet

by Walt Whitman

"And I or you pocketless of a dime
may purchase the pick of the earth."

Who troubles himself about his ornaments or fluency is lost. This is what you shall do: Love the earth and sun and the animals, despise riches, give alms to every one that asks, stand up for the stupid and crazy, devote your income and labor to others, hate tyrants, argue not concerning God, have patience and indulgence toward the people, take off your hat to nothing known or unknown or to any man or number of men, go freely with powerful uneducated persons and with the young and with the mothers of families, read these leaves in the open air every season of every year of your life, re-examine all you have been told at school or church or in any book, dismiss whatever insults your own soul, and your very flesh shall be a great poem and have the richest fluency not only in its words but in the silent lines of its lips and face and between the lashes of your eyes and in every motion and joint of your body. ...

The art of art, the glory of expression and the sunshine of the light of letters is simplicity. Nothing is better than simplicity . . . . nothing can make up for excess or for the lack of definiteness. To carry on the heave of impulse and pierce intellectual depths and give all subjects their articulations are powers neither common nor very uncommon. But to speak in literature with the perfect rectitude and insousiance of the movements of animals and the unimpeachableness of the sentiment of trees in the woods and grass by the roadside is the flawless triumph of art. If you have looked on him who has achieved it you have looked on one of the masters of the artists of all nations and times. You shall not contemplate the flight of the graygull over the bay or the mettlesome action of the blood horse or the tall leaning of sunflowers on their stalk or the appearance of the sun journeying through heaven or the appearance of the moon afterward with any more satisfaction than you shall contemplate him. The greatest poet has less a marked style and is more the channel of thoughts and things without increase or diminution, and is the free channel of himself. He swears to his art, I will not be meddlesome, I will not have in my writing any elegance or effect or originality to hang in the way between me and the rest like curtains. I will have nothing hang in the way, not the richest curtains. What I tell I tell for precisely what it is. Let who may exalt or startle or fascinate or sooth I will have purposes as health or heat or snow has and be as regardless of observation. What I experience or portray shall go from my composition without a shred of my composition. You shall stand by my side and look in the mirror with me. ...

The attitude of great poets is to cheer up slaves and horrify despots. ...

Great genius and the people of these states must never be demeaned to romances. As soon as histories are properly told there is no more need of romances.

The great poets are also to be known by the absence in them of tricks and by the justification of perfect personal candor. Then folks echo a new cheap joy and a divine voice leaping from their brains: How beautiful is candor! All faults may be forgiven of him who has perfect candor. Henceforth let no man of us lie, for we have seen that openness wins the inner and outer world and that there is no single exception, and that never since our earth gathered itself in a mass have deceit or subterfuge or prevarication attracted its smallest particle or the faintest tinge of a shade—and that through the enveloping wealth and rank of a state or the whole republic of states a sneak or sly person shall be discovered and despised . . . . and that the soul has never been once fooled and never can be fooled . . . . and thrift without the loving nod of the soul is only a foetid puff . . . . and there never grew up in any of the continents of the globe nor upon any planet or satellite or star, nor upon the asteroids, nor in any part of ethereal space, nor in the midst of density, nor under the fluid wet of the sea, nor in that condition which precedes the birth of babes, nor at any time during the changes of life, nor in that condition that follows what we term death, nor in any stretch of abeyance or action afterward of vitality, nor in any process of formation or reformation anywhere, a being whose instinct hated the truth.

§

After continued personal ambition and effort, as a young fellow, to enter with the rest into competition for the usual rewards, business, political, literary, &c. — to take part in the great mêlée, both for victory's prize itself and to do some good — After years of those aims and pursuits, I found myself remaining possess'd, at the age of thirty-one to thirty-three, with a special desire and conviction. Or rather, to be quite exact, a desire that had been flitting through my previous life, or hovering on the flanks, mostly indefinite hitherto, had steadily advanced to the front, defined itself, and finally dominated everything else. This was a feeling or ambition to articulate and faithfully express in literary or poetic form, and uncompromisingly, my own physical, emotional, moral, intellectual, and aesthetic Personality, in the midst of, and tallying, the momentous spirit and facts of its immediate days, and of current America — and to exploit that Personality identified with place and date, in a far more candid and comprehensive sense than any hitherto poem or book. ...

It is certainly time for America, above all, to begin this readjustment in the scope and basic point of view of verse; for everything else has changed. As I write, I see in an article on Wordsworth, in one of the current English magazines, the lines, "A few weeks ago an eminent French critic said that, owing to the special tendency to science and to its all-devouring force, poetry would cease to be read in fifty years." But I anticipate the very contrary. Only a firmer, vastly broader, new area begins to exist — nay, is already form'd — to which the poetic genius must emigrate. Whatever may have been the case in years gone by, the true use for the imaginative faculty of modern times is to give ultimate vivification to facts, to science, and to common lives, endowing them with the glows and glories and final illustriousness which belong to every real thing, and to real things only. Without that ultimate vivification — which the poet or other artist alone can give — reality would seem incomplete, and science, democracy, and life itself, finally in vain. ...

But I set out with the intention also of indicating or hinting some point-characteristics which I since see (though I did not then, at least not definitely) were bases and object-urgings toward those "Leaves" from the first. The word I myself put primarily for the description of them as they stand at last, is the word Suggestiveness. I round and finish little, if anything; and could not, consistently with my scheme. The reader will always have his or her part to do, just as much as I have had mine. I seek less to state or display any theme or thought, and more to bring you, reader, into the atmosphere of the theme or thought — there to pursue your own flight. Another impetus-word is Comradeship as for all lands, and in a more commanding and acknowledg'd sense than hitherto. Other word-signs would be Good Cheer, Content, and Hope.

The chief trait of any given poet is always the spirit he brings to the observation of Humanity and Nature — the mood out of which he contemplates his subjects. What kind of temper and what amount of faith report these things? Up to how recent a date is the song carried? What the equipment, and special raciness of the singer — what his tinge of coloring? The last value of artistic expressers, past and present — Greek aesthetes, Shakspere — or in our own day Tennyson, Victor Hugo, Carlyle, Emerson — is certainly involv'd in such questions. I say the profoundest service that poems or any other writings can do for their reader is not merely to satisfy the intellect, or supply something polish'd and interesting, nor even to depict great passions, or persons or events, but to fill him with vigorous and clean manliness, religiousness, and give him good heart as a radical possession and habit. The educated world seems to have been growing more and more ennuyed for ages, leaving to our time the inheritance of it all. Fortunately there is the original inexhaustible fund of buoyancy, normally resident in the race, forever eligible to be appeal'd to and relied on. ...

From another point of view "Leaves of Grass" is avowedly the song of Sex and Amativeness, and even Animality — though meanings that do not usually go along with those words are behind all, and will duly emerge; and all are sought to be lifted into a different light and atmosphere. Of this feature, intentionally palpable in a few lines, I shall only say the espousing principle of those lines so gives breath of life to my whole scheme that the bulk of the pieces might as well have been left unwritten were those lines omitted. Difficult as it will be, it has become, in my opinion, imperative to achieve a shifted attitude from superior men and women towards the thought and fact of sexuality, as an element in character, personality, the emotions, and a theme in literature. I am not going to argue the question by itself; it does not stand by itself. The vitality of it is altogether in its relations, bearings, significance — like the clef of a symphony. At last analogy the lines I allude to, and the spirit in which they are spoken, permeate all "Leaves of Grass," and the work must stand or fall with them, as the human body and soul must remain as an entirety. ...

As the present is perhaps mainly an attempt at personal statement or illustration, I will allow myself as further help to extract the following anecdote from a book, "Annals of Old Painters," conn'd by me in youth. Rubens, the Flemish painter, in one of his wanderings through the galleries of old convents, came across a singular work. After looking at it thoughtfully for a good while, and listening to the criticisms of his suite of students, he said to the latter, in answer to their questions (as to what school the work implied or belong'd,) "I do not believe the artist, unknown and perhaps no longer living, who has given the world this legacy, ever belong'd to any school, or ever painted anything but this one picture, which is a personal affair — a piece out of a man's life."

"Leaves of Grass" indeed (I cannot too often reiterate) has mainly been the outcropping of my own emotional and other personal nature — an attempt, from first to last, to put *a Person,* a human being (myself, in the latter half of the Nineteenth Century, in America,) freely, fully and truly on record. I could not find any similar personal record in current literature that satisfied me. But it is not on "Leaves of Grass" distinctively as *literature,* or a specimen thereof, that I feel to dwell, or advance claims. No one will get at my verses who insists upon viewing them as a literary performance, or attempt at such performance, or as aiming mainly toward art or æstheticism.

I say no land or people or circumstances ever existed so needing a race of singers and poems differing from all others, and rigidly their own, as the land and people and circumstances of our United States need such singers and poems to-day, and for the future. ...

Concluding with two items for the imaginative genius of the West, when it worthily rises — First, what Herder taught to the young Goethe, that really great poetry is always (like the Homeric or Biblical canticles) the result of a national spirit, and not the privilege of a polish'd and select few; Second, that the strongest and sweetest songs yet remain to be sung.

27
The Artist–Philosophers

by George Bernard Shaw

That the author of Everyman was no mere artist, but an artist-philosopher, and that the artist-philosophers are the only sort of artists I take quite seriously, will be no news to you. Even Plato and Boswell, as the dramatists who invented Socrates and Dr Johnson, impress me more deeply than the romantic playwrights. Ever since, as a boy, I first breathed the air of the transcendental regions at a performance of Mozart's *Zauberflöte [The Magic Flute],* I have been proof against the garish splendors and alcoholic excitements of the ordinary stage combinations of Tappertitian romance with the police intelligence. Bunyan, Blake, Hogarth and Turner (these four apart and above all the English Classics), Goethe, Shelley, Schopenhaur, Wagner, Ibsen, Morris, Tolstoy, and Nietzsche are among the writers whose peculiar sense of the world I recognize as more or less akin to my own. Mark the word peculiar. I read Dickens and Shakespear without shame or stint; but their pregnant observations and demonstrations of life are not co-ordinated into any philosophy or religion: on the contrary, Dickens's sentimental assumptions are violently contradicted by his observations; and Shakespear's pessimism is only his wounded humanity. Both have the specific genius of the fictionist and the common sympathies of human feeling and thought in pre-eminent degree. They are often saner and shrewder than the philosophers just as Sancho-Panza was often saner and shrewder than Don Quixote. They clear away vast masses of oppressive gravity by their sense of the ridiculous, which is at bottom a combination of sound moral judgment with lighthearted good humor. But they are concerned with the diversities of the world instead of with its unities: they are so irreligious that they exploit popular religion for professional purposes without delicacy or scruple (for example, Sydney Carton and the ghost in Hamlet!): they are anarchical, and cannot balance their exposures of Angelo and Dogberry, Sir Leicester Dedlock and Mr Tite Barnacle, with any portrait of a prophet or a worthy leader: they have no constructive ideas: they regard those who have them as dangerous fanatics: in all their fictions there is no leading thought or inspiration for which any man could conceivably risk the spoiling of his hat in a shower, much less his life. Both are alike forced to borrow motives for the more strenuous actions of their personages from the common stockpot of melodramatic plots; so that Hamlet has to be stimulated by the prejudices of a policeman and Macbeth by the cupidities of a bushranger. Dickens, without the excuse of having to manufacture motives for Hamlets and Macbeths, superfluously punts his crew down the stream of his monthly parts by mechanical devices which I leave you to describe, my own memory being quite baffled by the simplest question as to Monks in Oliver Twist, or the long lost parentage of Smike, or the relations between the Dorrit and Clennam families so inopportunely discovered by Monsieur Rigaud Blandois. The truth is, the world was to Shakespear a great "stage of fools" on which he was utterly bewildered. He could see no sort of sense in living at all; and Dickens saved himself from the despair of the dream in The Chimes by taking the world for granted and busying himself with its details. Neither of them could do anything with a serious positive character: they could place a human figure before you with perfect verisimilitude; but when the moment came for making it live and move, they found, unless it made them laugh, that they had a puppet on their hands, and had to invent some artificial external stimulus to make it work. This is what is the matter with Hamlet all through: he has no will except in his bursts of temper. Foolish Bardolaters make a virtue of this after their fashion: they declare that the play is the tragedy of irresolution; but all Shakespear's projections of the deepest humanity he knew have the same defect: their characters and manners are lifelike; but their actions are forced on them from without, and the external force is grotesquely inappropriate except when it is quite conventional, as in the case of Henry V. Falstaff is more vivid than any of these serious reflective characters, because he is self-acting: his motives are his own appetites and instincts and humors. Richard III, too, is delightful as the whimsical comedian who stops a funeral to make love to the corpse's widow; but when, in the next act, he is replaced by a stage villain who smothers babies and offs with people's heads, we are revolted at the imposture and repudiate the changeling. Faulconbridge, Coriolanus, Leontes are admirable descriptions of instinctive temperaments: indeed the play of Coriolanus is the greatest of Shakespear's comedies; but description is not philosophy; and comedy neither compromises the author nor reveals him. He must be judged by those characters into which he puts what he knows of himself, his Hamlets and Macbeths and Lears and Prosperos. If these characters are agonizing in a void about factitious melodramatic murders and revenges and the like, whilst the comic characters walk with their feet on solid ground, vivid and amusing, you know that the author has much to show and nothing to teach. The comparison between Falstaff and Prospero is like the comparison between Micawber and David Copperfield. At the end of the book you know Micawber, whereas you only know what has happened to David, and are not interested enough in him to wonder what his politics or religion might be if anything so stupendous as a religious or political idea, or a general idea of any sort, were to occur to him. He is tolerable as a child; but he never becomes a man, and might be left out of his own biography altogether but for his usefulness as a stage confidant, a Horatio or "Charles his friend": what they call on the stage a feeder.

Now you cannot say this of the works of the artist-philosophers. You cannot say it, for instance, of The Pilgrim's Progress. Put your Shakespearian hero and coward, Henry V and Pistol or Parolles, beside Mr Valiant and Mr Fearing, and you have a sudden revelation of the abyss that lies between the fashionable author who could see nothing in the world but personal aims and the tragedy of their disappointment or the comedy of their incongruity, and the field preacher who achieved virtue and courage by identifying himself with the purpose of the world as he understood it. The contrast is enormous: Bunyan's coward stirs your blood more than Shakespear's hero, who actually leaves you cold and secretly hostile. You suddenly see that Shakespear, with all his flashes and divinations, never understood virtue and courage, never conceived how any man who was not a fool could, like Bunyan's hero, look back from the brink of the river of death over the strife and labor of his pilgrimage, and say "yet do I not repent me"; or, with the panache of a millionaire, bequeath "my sword to him that shall succeed me in my pilgrimage, and my courage and skill to him that can get it." This is the true joy in life, the being used for a purpose recognized by yourself as a mighty one; the being thoroughly worn out before you are thrown on the scrap heap; the being a force of Nature instead of a feverish selfish little clod of ailments and grievances complaining that the world will not devote itself to making you happy. And also the only real tragedy in life is the being used by personally minded men for purposes which you recognize to be base. All the rest is at worst mere misfortune or mortality: this alone is misery, slavery, hell on earth; and the revolt against it is the only force that offers a man's work to the poor artist, whom our personally minded rich people would so willingly employ as pandar, buffoon, beauty monger, sentimentalizer and the like.

It may seem a long step from Bunyan to Nietzsche; but the difference between their conclusions is purely formal. Bunyan's perception that righteousness is filthy rags, his scorn for Mr Legality in the village of Morality, his defiance of the Church as the supplanter of religion, his insistence on courage as the virtue of virtues, his estimate of the career of the conventionally respectable and sensible Worldly Wiseman as no better at bottom than the life and death of Mr Badman: all this, expressed by Bunyan in the terms of a tinker's theology, is what Nietzsche has expressed in terms of post-Darwinian, post-Schopenhaurian philosophy; Wagner in terms of polytheistic mythology; and Ibsen in terms of mid-XIX century Parisian dramaturgy. Nothing is new in these matters except their novelties: for instance, it is a novelty to call Justification by Faith "Wille," and Justification by Works "Vorstellung." The sole use of the novelty is that you and I buy and read Schopenhaur's treatise on Will and Representation when we should not dream of buying a set of sermons on Faith versus Works. At bottom the controversy is the same, and the dramatic results are the same. Bunyan makes no attempt to present his pilgrims as more sensible or better conducted than Mr Worldly Wiseman. Mr W. W.'s worst enemies, as Mr Embezzler, Mr Never-go-to-Church-on-Sunday, Mr Bad Form, Mr Murderer, Mr Burglar, Mr Co-respondent, Mr Blackmailer, Mr Cad, Mr Drunkard, Mr Labor Agitator and so forth, can read the Pilgrim's Progress without finding a word said against them; whereas the respectable people who snub them and put them in prison, such as Mr W.W. himself and his young friend Civility; Formalist and Hypocrisy; Wildhead, Inconsiderate, and Pragmatick (who were clearly young university men of good family and high feeding); that brisk lad Ignorance, Talkative, By-Ends of Fairspeech and his mother-in-law Lady Feigning, and other reputable gentlemen and citizens, catch it very severely. Even Little Faith, though he gets to heaven at last, is given to understand that it served him right to be mobbed by the brothers Faint Heart, Mistrust, and Guilt, all three recognized members of respectable society and veritable pillars of the law. The whole allegory is a consistent attack on morality and respectability, without a word that one can remember against vice and crime. Exactly what is complained of in Nietzsche and Ibsen, is it not? And also exactly what would be complained of in all the literature which is great enough and old enough to have attained canonical rank, officially or unofficially, were it not that books are admitted to the canon by a compact which confesses their greatness in consideration of abrogating their meaning; so that the reverend rector can agree with the prophet Micah as to his inspired style without being committed to any complicity in Micah's furiously Radical opinions. Why, even I, as I force myself, pen in hand, into recognition and civility, find all the force of my onslaught destroyed by a simple policy of non-resistance. In vain do I redouble the violence of the language in which I proclaim my heterodoxies. I rail at the theistic credulity of Voltaire, the amoristic superstition of Shelley, the revival of tribal soothsaying and idolatrous rites which Huxley called Science and mistook for an advance on the Pentateuch, no less than at the welter of ecclesiastical and professional humbug which saves the face of the stupid system of violence and robbery which we call Law and Industry. Even atheists reproach me with infidelity and anarchists with nihilism because I cannot endure their moral tirades. And yet, instead of exclaiming "Send this inconceivable Satanist to the stake," the respectable newspapers pith me by announcing "another book by this brilliant and thoughtful writer." And the ordinary citizen, knowing that an author who is well spoken of by a respectable newspaper must be all right, reads me, as he reads Micah, with undisturbed edification from his own point of view. It is narrated that in the eighteen-seventies an old lady, a very devout Methodist, moved from Colchester to a house in the neighborhood of the City Road, in London, where, mistaking the Hall of Science for a chapel, she sat at the feet of Charles Bradlaugh for many years, entranced by his eloquence, without questioning his orthodoxy or moulting a feather of her faith. I fear I small be defrauded of my just martyrdom in the same way.

However, I am digressing, as a man with a grievance always does. And after all, the main thing in determining the artistic quality of a book is not the opinions it propagates, but the fact that the writer has opinions. The old lady from Colchester was right to sun her simple soul in the energetic radiance of Bradlaugh's genuine beliefs and disbeliefs rather than in the chill of such mere painting of light and heat as elocution and convention can achieve. My contempt for *belles lettres,* and for amateurs who become the heroes of the fanciers of literary virtuosity, is not founded on any illusion of mind as to the permanence of those forms of thought (call them opinions) by which I strive to communicate my bent to my fellows. To younger men they are already outmoded; for though they have no more lost their logic than an eighteenth century pastel has lost its drawing or its color, yet, like the pastel, they grow indefinably shabby, and will grow shabbier until they cease to count at all, when my books will either perish, or, if the world is still poor enough to want them, will have to stand, with Bunyan's, by quite amorphous qualities of temper and energy. With this conviction I cannot be a bellettrist. No doubt I must recognize, as even the Ancient Mariner did, that I must tell my story entertainingly if I am to hold the wedding guest spellbound in spite of the siren sounds of the loud bassoon. But "for art's sake" alone I would not face the toil of writing a single sentence. I know that there are men who, having nothing to say and nothing to write, are nevertheless so in love with oratory and with literature that they keep desperately repeating as much as they can understand of what others have said or written aforetime. I know that the leisurely tricks which their want of conviction leaves them free to play with the diluted and misapprehended message supply them with a pleasant parlor game which they call style. I can pity their dotage and even sympathize with their fancy. But a true original style is never achieved for its own sake: a man may pay from a shilling to a guinea, according to his means, to see, hear, or read another man's act of genius; but he will not pay with his whole life and soul to become a mere virtuoso in literature, exhibiting an accomplishment which will not even make money for him, like fiddle playing. Effectiveness of assertion is the Alpha and Omega of style. He who has nothing to assert has no style and can have none: he who has something to assert will go as far in power of style as its momentousness and his conviction will carry him. Disprove his assertion after it is made, yet its style remains. Darwin has no more destroyed the style of Job nor of Handel than Martin Luther destroyed the style of Giotto. All the assertions get disproved sooner or later; and so we find the world full of a magnificent debris of artistic fossils, with the matter-of-fact credibility gone clean out of them, but the form still splendid. And that is why the old masters play the deuce with our mere susceptibles. Your Royal Academician thinks he can get the style of Giotto without Giotto's beliefs, and correct his perspective into the bargain. Your man of letters thinks he can get Bunyan's or Shakespear's style without Bunyan's conviction or Shakespear's apprehension, especially if he takes care not to split his infinitives. And so with your Doctors of Music, who, with their collections of discords duly prepared and resolved or retarded or anticipated in the manner of the great composers, think they can learn the art of Palestrina from Cherubim's treatise. All this academic art is far worse than the trade in sham antique furniture; for the man who sells me an oaken chest which he swears was made in the XIII century, though as a matter of fact he made it himself only yesterday, at least does not pretend that there are any modern ideas in it, whereas your academic copier of fossils offers them to you as the latest outpouring of the human spirit, and, worst of all, kidnaps young people as pupils and persuades them that his limitations are rules, his observances dexterities, his timidities good taste, and his emptinesses purities. And when he declares that art should not be didactic, all the people who have nothing to teach and all the people who don't want to learn agree with him emphatically.

I pride myself on not being one of these susceptible: If you study the electric light with which I supply you in that Bumbledonian public capacity of mine over which you make merry from time to time, you will find that your house contains a great quantity of highly susceptible copper wire which gorges itself with electricity and gives you no light whatever. But here and there occurs a scrap of intensely insusceptible, intensely resistant material; and that stubborn scrap grapples with the current and will not let it through until it has made itself useful to you as those two vital qualities of literature, light and heat. Now if I am to be no mere copper wire amateur but a luminous author, I must also be a most intensely refractory person, liable to go out and to go wrong at inconvenient moments, and with incendiary possibilities. These are the faults of my qualities; and I assure you that

I sometimes dislike myself so much that when some irritable reviewer chances at that moment to pitch into me with zest, I feel unspeakably relieved and obliged. But I never dream of reforming, knowing that I must take myself as I am and get what work I can out of myself. All this you will understand; for there is community of material between us: we are both critics of life as well as of art; and you have perhaps said to yourself when I have passed your windows, "There, but for the grace of God, go I." An awful and chastening reflection, which shall be the closing cadence of this immoderately long letter from yours faithfully,

G. Bernard Shaw
Woking, 1903

28
The Art of Style

by John Addington Symonds

I

"The choice and command of language," said Gibbon, "is the fruit of exercise." Every writer has it in his power to improve his faculty of expression, as every athlete can improve his muscular development by practice.

The final end of all style is precision, veracity of utterance, truth to the thing to be presented. The thing itself will differ in simplicity and complexity, in scientific aridity and in emotional richness, in imaginative grandeur and in passionate intensity. Style, regarded from the point of view of art, adapts itself to these differences in subject-matter. Whether consciously or unconsciously, is not at present the question. It suffices to say that style (if worthy of the name) finds the pure phrase the fitting mode of utterance. It rejects superfluities, admits ornament where ornament is part and parcel of the thing to be presented, seeks beauty in truth, selects, discards, mindful always that there is one and only one absolutely right way of saying anything.

This is true of poetry as of prose. Phrases like:

> Thou dost preserve the stars from wrong;
> And the most ancient heavens, through Thee, are fresh and strong;

or like:
> Make me thy lyre, even as the forest is;
> What if my leaves are falling like its own!

have to be regarded as simple propositions, no less simple than these which follow:
> So ended this great siege, the most memorable in the annals of the British Isles. It had lasted a hundred and five days. The garrison had been reduced from about seven thousand effective men to about three thousand.

All these propositions are right, are veracious, are good in style, in so far as they are adequate to the speaker's thought and perception of fact – in the first two cases to the highly charged and complex matter which Wordsworth and Shelley sought to deliver, and in the third to the definite issue which Macaulay had to report. Criticism might question whether the siege of Londonderry was really "the most memorable in the annals of the British Isles." But criticism, knowing Macaulay's view of English history, would have no right to challenge his statement on the ground of style. Criticism might object to Wordsworth's indentification of Duty with Cosmic Law, and to Shelley's pathetic sympathy with autumn woodlands. But criticism, having seized each poet's point of view, would have no right to challenge his statement on the ground of style. In each case the verbal expression is correspondent to the thing presented.

Precision being the main purpose of a writer, he will pay minute attention to the grammar and logic of language, so that there may be no obscurity, or incoherence in his method of expression. With the same object he will study the qualities of words, remembering that the right word used in the right place constitutes the perfection of style. Words will be weighed in their sonority, their colour-value, their suggestiveness, their derivation and metaphysical usage. He will show his taste by the avoidance of foreign vocables, neologisms, obsolete terms, unless the rhetoric of his subject-matter renders such *verba insolentia* helpful to the meaning. To be meticulous (as Sir Thomas Browne would say), in the adoption of new phrases or the resuscitation of old words is hardly less reprehensible than to be reckless in the ill-considered use of them. Justice of perception consists in knowing how and when and where to deviate from the beaten track; and in nothing do writers of equal excellence reveal their individual proclivities more plainly than in their selection of uncommon vocables or turns of phrase.

The art of style, like all arts of expression, does not aim exclusively at precision. It is a fine art, and demands beauty as the concomitant of truth. We have a sense for the beauty of language in itself, just as we have a sense for the beauty of sounds, colours, forms. This sense claims to be gratified by harmonious and rhythmic utterance. Students of style will therefore take pains to avoid unnecessary tautology, to vary the openings and outlines of propositions, to alternate long and short sentences, and to connect these into well-built paragraphs. They will be sensible that, as every idea has its one right verbal form, so every phrase ought to have its own distinctive cadence. Goethe used to say that each poetic motive brought with it a rhythm and a stanza proper to itself; and this remark might be extended to the minutest particles of thought conveyed in language.

Only slovenly writers who never felt the beauty of verbal form, and brutal writers who do wilful violence to the langauge, ignore the duty of seeking the right phrase. Those for whom style is an art will differ immeasurably in their power to use it. The unknown painter struggling with a task beyond his faculty cannot charm our senses with the suave and luminous achievements of a Titian or Veronese. But even humble workers are able to do much by love and care, toward lifting their utterance above the dead level of the commonplace. Let them write sentences, recast paragraphs, remould chapters, seeking at every step a bettering of their best, a closer union with the melody which penetrates the intellectual ear. Striving thus, we become sensible of what is meant by art in style. We grow more vigorous; and when there comes some vital thought to utter, the clothing words spring forth with more of freshness, strength, and music.

The lucid exposition of ideas in ordered sequence, the weaving of sentences into coherent paragraphs, the unfolding of arguments by natural yet logically constructed steps, the presentation of scenes and pictures by successions of contributory images – these operations of the literary craftsman demand close attention to what is called transition. Style, it has been said, consists in the art of transition: that is, the art of moving easily and convincingly from point to point, supplying the needful "connective tissue" of language without clumsiness and without the obstrusive pedantry of scholastic distinctions. Nor let it be imagined that this is a mere matter of stylistic grace. The art of transition and connection has quite as much to do with veracity of thought as with elegance of expression. It was upon this art, as the one thing needful to sound rhetoric, that Socrates discoursed in his golden way to Phaedrus on the banks of the Ilissus. This is what Buffon meant by the words which so impressed Gustave Flaubert: "Toutes les beautés intellectuelles qui se trouvent dans un beau style, tous les rapports dont il est composé, sont autant de vérités aussi utiles, et peut-être plus précieuses pour l'esprit public, que celles qui peuvent faire le fond du sujet." [The intellectual refinements of a distinguished style, its careful proportions, have as much their actual value to the general understanding as the underlying ideas, and may perhaps be more highly prized.]

II

When bestowing minute attention on the niceties of language, young writers should bear in mind that no rules of composition, no rhetoric which professes to teach the art of treating subjects appropriately, can supply the two requisites of a good style – vigorous and well-digested thought, which constitutes its matter; and pure idiomatic diction, which constitutes its crowning grace and form.

"Authors," said De Quincey, in his unfinished essay on Style, "have always been a dangerous class for any language." They have been dangerous because they are liable to substitute sophistry and declamation for solid thinking, and because of the habit of writing books alienates their language from the vivacity of the vernacular and the raciness of spoken idiom.

Few men of letters nowadays would dare to follow Swift and Sterne, those classics of our prose, in their bold use of colloquialisms. Goethe prided himself on "having never thought much about thinking." We might argue in favor of not thinking overmuch about writing. A fastidious avoidance of what is plain and common may lead us insensibly into the worst of all faults − affectation and stylistic pedantry; may blind us to the fact that what we say is more important than how we say it, and that the first condition of good writing is strong feeling and clear thinking.

Englishmen, however, incline toward carelessness rather than scrupulousness in the matter of language. It will be long before our journalists and novelists deserve the reporach which George Sand is said to have addressed Flaubert, and which, in my opinion, Flaubert, that martyr to verbal nicety, deserved: "You regard expression as an end in itself; it is but an effect."

29
On Familiar Style

by William Hazlitt

It is not easy to write a familiar style. Many people mistake a familiar for a vulgar style, and suppose that to write without affectation is to write at random. On the contrary, there is nothing that requires more precision, and, if I may so say, purity of expression, than the style I am speaking of. It utterly rejects not only all unmeaning pomp, but all low, cant phrases, and loose, unconnected, *slipshod* allusions. It is not to take the first word that offers, but the best word in common use; it is not to throw words together in any combinations we please, but to follow and avail ourselves of the true idiom of the language. To write a genuine familiar or truly English style is to write as anyone would speak in common conversation who had a thorough command and choice of words, or who could discourse with ease, force, and perspicuity, setting aside all pedantic and oratorical flourishes. Or, to give another illustration, to write naturally is the same thing in regard to common conversation as to read naturally is in regard to common speech. It does not follow that it is an easy thing to give the true accent and inflection to the words you utter, because you do not attempt to rise above the level of ordinary life and colloquial speaking. You do not assume, indeed, the solemnity of the pulpit, or the tone of stage-declamation; neither are you at liberty to gabble on at a venture, without emphasis or discretion, or to resort to vulgar dialect or clownish pronunciation. You must steer a middle course. You are tied down to a given and appropriate articulation, which is determined by the habitual associations between sense and sound, and which you can only hit by entering into the author's meaning, as you must find the proper words and style to express yourself by fixing your thoughts on the subject you have to write about. Anyone may mouth out a passage with a theatrical cadence, or get upon stilts to tell his thoughts; but to write or speak with propriety and simplicity is a more difficult task. Thus it is easy to affect a pompous style, to use a word twice as big as the thing you want to express: it is not so easy to pitch upon the very word that exactly fits it. Out of eight or ten words equally common, equally intelligible, with nearly equal pretensions, it is a matter of some nicety and discrimination to pick out the very one the preferableness of which is scarcely perceptible, but decisive. The reason why I object to Dr. Johnson's style is that there is no discrimination, no selection, no variety in it. He uses none but 'tall, opaque words,' taken from the 'first row of the rubric'—words with the greatest number of syllables, or Latin phrases with merely English terminations. If a fine style depended on this sort of arbitrary pretension, it would be fair to judge of an author's elegance by the measurement of his words and the substitution of foreign circumlocutions (with no precise associations) for the mother-tongue.{1} How simple is it to be dignified without ease, to be pompous without meaning! Surely, it is but a mechanical rule for avoiding what is low, to be always pedantic and affected. It is clear you cannot use a vulgar English word if you never use a common English word at all. A fine tact is shown in adhering to those which are perfectly common, and yet never falling into any expressions which are debased by disgusting circumstances, or which owe their signification and point to technical or professional allusions. A truly natural or familiar style can never be quaint or vulgar, for this reason, that it is of universal force and applicability, and that quaintness and vulgarity arise out of the immediate connection of certain words with coarse and disagreeable, or with confined ideas. The last form what we understand by *cant* or *slang* phrases.–To give an example of what is not very clear in the general statement, I should say that the phrase *To cut with a knife*, or *To cut a piece of wood,* is perfectly free from vulgarity, because it is perfectly common; but *to cut an acquaintance* is not quite unexceptionable, because it is not perfectly common or intelligible, and has hardly yet escaped out of the limits of slang phraseology. I should hardly, therefore, use the word in this sense without putting it in italics as a license of expression, to be received *cum grano salis.*{2} All provincial or bye-phrases come under the same mark of reprobation—all such as the writer transfers to the page from his fireside or a particular *coterie,* or that he invents for his own sole use and convenience. I conceive that words are like money, not the worse for being common, but that it is the stamp of custom alone that gives them circulation or value. I am fastidious in this respect, and would almost as soon coin the currency of the realm as counterfeit the King's English. I never invented or gave a new and unauthorised meaning to any word but one single one (the term *impersonal* applied to feelings), and that was in an abstruse metaphysical discussion to express a very difficult distinction. I have been (I know) loudly accused of revelling in vulgarisms and broken English. I cannot speak to that point; but so far I plead guilty to the determined use of acknowledged idioms and common elliptical expressions. I am not sure that the critics in question know the one from the other, that is, can distinguish any medium between formal pedantry and the most barbarous solecism. As an author I endeavour to employ plain words and popular modes of construction, as, were I a chapman and dealer, I should common weights and measures.

Notes to *On Familiar Style* by William Hazlitt

1. I have heard of such a thing as an author who makes it a rule never to admit a monosyllable into his vapid verse. Yet the charm and sweetness of Marlowe's lines depended often on their being made up almost entirely of monosyllables. (WH)

2. *cum grano salis* (Latin, "with a grain of salt") — be skeptical about the story or statement. (MP)

30
On Thinking for Oneself

by Arthur Schopenhauer

A library may be very large; but if it is in disorder, it is not so useful as one that is small but well arranged. In the same way, a man may have a great mass of knowledge, but if he has not worked it up by thinking it over for himself, it has much less value than a far smaller amount which he has thoroughly pondered. For it is only when a man looks at his knowledge from all sides, and combines the things he knows by comparing truth with truth, that he obtains a complete hold over it and gets it into his power. A man cannot turn over anything in his mind unless he knows it; he should, therefore, learn something; but it is only when he has turned it over that he can be said to know it.

Reading and learning are things that anyone can do of his own free will; but not so *thinking*. Thinking must be kindled, like a fire by a draught; it must be sustained by some interest in the matter in hand. This interest may be of purely objective kind, or merely subjective. The latter comes into play only in things that concern us personally. Objective interest is confined to heads that think by nature; to whom thinking is as natural as breathing; and they are very rare. This is why most men of learning show so little of it.

It is incredible what a different effect is produced upon the mind by thinking for oneself, as compared with reading. It carries on and intensifies that original difference in the nature of two minds which leads the one to think and the other to read. What I mean is that reading forces alien thoughts upon the mind—thoughts which are as foreign to the drift and temper in which it may be for the moment, as the seal is to the wax on which it stamps its imprint. The mind is thus entirely under compulsion from without; it is driven to think this or that, though for the moment it may not have the slightest impulse or inclination to do so.

But when a man thinks for himself, he follows the impulse of his own mind, which is determined for him at the time, either by his environment or some particular recollection. The visible world of a man's surroundings does not, as reading does, impress a *single* definite thought upon his mind, but merely gives the matter and occasion which lead him to think what is appropriate to his nature and present temper. So it is, that much reading deprives the mind of all elasticity; it is like keeping a spring continually under pressure. The safest way of having no thoughts of one's own is to take up a book every moment one has nothing else to do. It is this practice which explains why erudition makes most men more stupid and silly than they are by nature, and prevents their writings obtaining any measure of success. They remain, in Pope's words:

> *For ever reading, never to be read!* {1}

Men of learning are those who have done their reading in the pages of a book. Thinkers and men of genius are those who have gone straight to the book of Nature; it is they who have enlightened the world and carried humanity further on its way. If a man's thoughts are to have truth and life in them, they must, after all, be his own fundamental thoughts; for these are the only ones that he can fully and wholly understand. To read another's thoughts is like taking the leavings of a meal to which we have not been invited, or putting on the clothes which some unknown visitor has laid aside. The thought we read is related to the thought which springs up in ourselves, as the fossil-impress of some prehistoric plant to a plant as it buds forth in spring-time.

Reading is nothing more than a substitute for thought of one's own. It means putting the mind into leading-strings. The multitude of books serves only to show how many false paths there are, and how widely astray a man may wander if he follows any of them. But he who is guided by his genius, he who thinks for himself, who thinks spontaneously and exactly, possesses the only compass by which he can steer aright. A man should read only when his own thoughts stagnate at their source, which will happen often enough even with the best of minds. On the other hand, to take up a book for the purpose of scaring away one's own original thoughts is sin against the Holy Spirit. It is like running away from Nature to look at a museum of dried plants or gaze at a landscape in copperplate.

A man may have discovered some portion of truth or wisdom, after spending a great deal of time and trouble in thinking it over for himself and adding thought to thought; and it may sometimes happen that he could have found it all ready to hand in a book and spared himself the trouble. But even so, it is a hundred times more valuable if he has acquired it by thinking it out for himself. For it is only when we gain our knowledge in this way that it enters as an integral part, a living member, into the whole system of our thought; that it stands in complete and firm relation with what we know; that it is understood with all that underlies it and follows from it; that it wears the color, the precise shade, the distinguishing mark, of our own way of thinking; that it comes exactly at the right time, just as we felt the necessity for it; that it stands fast and cannot be forgotten. This is the perfect application, nay, the interpretation, of Goethe's advice to earn our inheritance for ourselves so that we may really possess it:

Was due ererbt von deinen Välern hast,
Erwirb es, um es zu besitzen. {2}

The man who thinks for himself, forms his own opinions and learns the authorities for them only later on, when they serve but to strengthen his belief in them and in himself. But the book-philosopher starts from the authorities. He reads other people's books, collects their opinions, and so forms a whole for himself, which resembles an automaton made up of anything but flesh and blood. Contrarily, he who thinks for himself creates a work like a living man as made by Nature. For the work comes into being as a man does; the thinking mind is impregnated from without, and it then forms and bears its child.

Truth that has been merely learned is like an artificial limb, a false tooth, a waxen nose; at best, like a nose made out of another's flesh; it adheres to us only because it is put on. But truth acquired by thinking of our own is like a natural limb; it alone really belongs to us. This is the fundamental difference between the thinker and the mere man of learning. The intellectual attainments of a man who thinks for himself resemble a fine painting, where the light and shade are correct, the tone sustained, the color perfectly harmonized; it is true to life. On the other hand, the intellectual attainments of the mere man of learning are like a large palette, full of all sorts of colors, which at most are systematically arranged, but devoid of harmony, connection and meaning.

Reading is thinking with some one else's head instead of one's own. To think with one's own head is always to aim at developing a coherent whole—a system, even though it be not a strictly complete one; and nothing hinders this so much as too strong a current of others' thoughts, such as comes of continual reading. These thoughts, springing every one of them from different minds, belonging to different systems, and tinged with different colors, never of themselves flow together into an intellectual whole; they never form a unity of knowledge, or insight, or conviction; but, rather, fill the head with a Babylonian confusion of tongues. The mind that is over-loaded with alien thought is thus deprived of all clear insight, and is well-nigh disorganized. This is a state of things observable in many men of learning; and it makes them inferior in sound sense, correct judgment and practical tact, to many illiterate persons, who, after obtaining a little knowledge from without, by means of experience, intercourse with others, and a small amount of reading, have always subordinated it to, and embodied it with, their own thought.

The really scientific *thinker* does the same thing as these illiterate persons, but on a larger scale. Although he has need of much knowledge, and so must read a great deal, his mind is nevertheless strong enough to master it all, to assimilate and incorporate it with the system of his thoughts, and so to make it fit in with the organic unity of his insight, which, though vast, is always growing. And in the process, his own thought, like the bass in an organ, always dominates everything and is never drowned by other tones, as happens with minds which are full of mere antiquarian lore; where shreds of music, as it were, in every key, mingle confusedly, and no fundamental note is heard at all.

Those who have spent their lives in reading, and taken their wisdom from books, are like people who have obtained precise information about a country from the descriptions of many travellers. Such people can tell a great deal about it; but, after all, they have no connected, clear, and profound knowledge of its real condition. But those who have spent their lives in thinking, resemble the travellers themselves; they alone really know what they are talking about; they are acquainted with the actual state of affairs, and are quite at home in the subject.

The thinker stands in the same relation to the ordinary book-philosopher as an eye-witness does to the historian; he speaks from direct knowledge of his own. That is why all those who think for themselves come, at bottom, to much the same conclusion. The differences they present are due to their different points of view; and when these do not affect the matter, they all speak alike. They merely express the result of their own objective perception of things. There are many passages in my works which I have given to the public only after some hesitation, because of their paradoxical nature; and afterwards I have experienced a pleasant surprise in finding the same opinion recorded in the works of great men who lived long ago.

The book-philosopher merely reports what one person has said and another meant, or the objections raised by a third, and so on. He compares different opinions, ponders, criticises, and tries to get at the truth of the matter; herein on a par with the critical historian. For instance, he will set out to inquire whether Leibnitz was not for some time a follower of Spinoza, and questions of a like nature. The curious student of such matters may find conspicuous examples of what I mean in Herbart's *Analytical Elucidation of Morality and Natural Right,* and in the same author's *Letters on Freedom.* Surprise may be felt that a man of the kind should put himself to so much trouble; for, on the face of it, if he would only examine the matter for himself, he would speedily attain his object by the exercise of a little thought. But there is a small difficulty in the way. It does not depend upon his own will. A man can always sit down and read, but not—think. It is with thoughts as with men; they cannot always be summoned at pleasure; we must wait for them to come. Thought about a subject must appear of itself, by a happy and harmonious combination of external stimulus with mental temper and attention; and it is just that which never seems to come to these people.

This truth may be illustrated by what happens in the case of matters affecting our own personal interest. When it is necessary to come to some resolution in a matter of that kind, we cannot well sit down at any given moment and think over the merits of the case and make up our mind; for, if we try to do so, we often find ourselves unable, at that particular moment, to keep our mind fixed upon the subject; it wanders off to other things. Aversion to the matter in question is sometimes to blame for this. In such a case we should not use force, but wait for the proper frame of mind to come of itself. It often comes unexpectedly and returns again and again; and the variety of temper in which we approach it at different moments puts the matter always in a fresh light. It is this long process which is understood by the term *a ripe resolution.* For the work of coming to a resolution must be distributed; and in the process much that is overlooked at one moment occurs to us at another; and the repugnance vanishes when we find, as we usually do, on a closer inspection, that things are not so bad as they seemed.

This rule applies to the life of the intellect as well as to matters of practice. A man must wait for the right moment. Not even the greatest mind is capable of thinking for itself at all times. Hence a great mind does well to spend its leisure in reading, which, as I have said, is a substitute for thought; it brings stuff to the mind by letting another person do the thinking; although that is always done in a manner not our own. Therefore, a man should not read too much, in order that his mind may not become accustomed to the substitute and thereby forget the reality; that it may not form the habit of walking in well-worn paths; nor by following an alien course of thought grow a stranger to its own. Least of all should a man quite withdraw his gaze from the real world for the mere sake of reading; as the impulse and the temper which prompt to thought of one's own come far oftener from the world of reality than from the world of books. The real life that a man sees before him is the natural subject of thought; and in its strength as the primary element of existence, it can more easily than anything else rouse and influence the thinking mind.

After these considerations, it will not be matter for surprise that a man who thinks for himself can easily be distinguished from the book-philosopher by the very way in which he talks, by his marked earnestness, and the originality, directness, and personal conviction that stamp all his thoughts and expressions. The book-philosopher, on the other hand, lets it be seen that everything he has is second-hand; that his ideas are like the number and trash of an old furniture-shop, collected together from all quarters. Mentally, he is dull and pointless—a copy of a copy. His literary style is made up of conventional, nay, vulgar phrases, and terms that happen to be current; in this respect much like a small State where all the money that circulates is foreign, because it has no coinage of its own.

Mere experience can as little as reading supply the place of thought. It stands to thinking in the same relation in which eating stands to digestion and assimilation. When experience boasts that to its discoveries alone is due the advancement of the human race, it is as though the mouth were to claim the whole credit of maintaining the body in health.

The works of all truly capable minds are distinguished by a character of *decision* and *definiteness,* which means they are clear and free from obscurity. A truly capable mind always knows definitely and clearly what it is that it wants to express, whether its medium is prose, verse, or music. Other minds are not decisive and not definite; and by this they may be known for what they are.

The characteristic sign of a mind of the highest order is that it always judges at first hand. Everything it advances is the result of thinking for itself; and this is everywhere evident by the way in which it gives its thoughts utterance. Such a mind is like a Prince. In the realm of intellect its authority is imperial, whereas the authority of minds of a lower order is delegated only; as may be seen in their style, which has no independent stamp of its own.

Every one who really thinks for himself is so far like a monarch. His position is undelegated and supreme. His judgments, like royal decrees, spring from his own sovereign power and proceed directly from himself. He acknowledges authority as little as a monarch admits a command; he subscribes to nothing but what he has himself authorized. The multitude of common minds, laboring under all sorts of current opinions, authorities, prejudices, is like the people, which silently obeys the law and accepts orders from above.

Those who are so zealous and eager to settle debated questions by citing authorities, are really glad when they are able to put the understanding and the insight of others into the field in place of their own, which are wanting. Their number is legion. For, as Seneca says, there is no man but prefers belief to the exercise of judgment—*unusquisque mavult credere quam judicare.* In their controversies such people make a promiscuous use of the weapon of authority, and strike out at one another with it. If any one chances to become involved in such a contest, he will do well not to try reason and argument as a mode of defence; for against a weapon of that kind these people are like Siegfrieds, with a skin of horn, and dipped in the flood of incapacity for thinking and judging. They will meet his attack by bringing up their authorities as a way of abashing him—*argumentum ad verecundiam,* and then cry out that they have won the battle.

In the real world, be it never so fair, favorable and pleasant, we always live subject to the law of gravity which we have to be constantly overcoming. But in the world of intellect we are disembodied spirits, held in bondage to no such law, and free from penury and distress. Thus it is that there exists no happiness on earth like that which, at the auspicious moment, a fine and fruitful mind finds in itself.

The presence of a thought is like the presence of a woman we love. We fancy we shall never forget the thought nor become indifferent to the dear one. But out of sight, out of mind! The finest thought runs the risk of being irrevocably forgotten if we do not write it down, and the darling of being deserted if we do not marry her.

There are plenty of thoughts which are valuable to the man who thinks them; but only few of them which have enough strength to produce repercussive or reflective action—I mean, to win the reader's sympathy after they have been put on paper.

But still it must not be forgotten that a true value attaches only to what a man has thought in the first instance *for his own case.* Thinkers may be classed according as they think chiefly for their own case or for that of others. The former are the genuine independent thinkers; they really think and are really independent; they are the true *philosophers;* they alone are in earnest. The pleasure and the happiness of their existence consists in thinking. The others are the *sophists;* they want to seem that which they are not, and seek their happiness in what they hope to get from the world. They are in earnest about nothing else. To which of these two classes a man belongs may be seen by his whole style and manner. Lichtenberg is an example for the former class; Herder, there can be no doubt, belongs to the second.

When one considers how vast and how close to us is *the problem of existence*—this equivocal, tortured, fleeting, dream-like existence of ours— so vast and so close that a man no sooner discovers it than it overshadows and obscures all other problems and aims; and when one sees how all men, with few and rare exceptions, have no clear consciousness of the problem, nay, seem to be quite unaware of its presence, but busy themselves with everything rather than with this, and live on, taking no thought but for the passing day and the hardly longer span of their own personal future, either expressly discarding the problem or else over-ready to come to terms with it by adopting some system of popular metaphysics and letting it satisfy them; when, I say, one takes all this to heart, one may come to the opinion that man may be said to be *a thinking being* only in a very remote sense, and henceforth feel no special surprise at any trait of human thoughtlessness or folly; but know, rather, that the normal man's intellectual range of vision does indeed extend beyond that of the brute, whose whole existence is, as it were, a continual present, with no consciousness of the past or the future, but not such an immeasurable distance as is generally supposed.

This is, in fact, corroborated by the way in which most men converse; where their thoughts are found to be chopped up fine, like chaff, so that for them to spin out a discourse of any length is impossible.

If this world were peopled by really thinking beings, it could not be that noise of every kind would be allowed such generous limits, as is the case with the most horrible and at the same time aimless form of it.{3} If Nature had meant man to think, she would not have given him ears; or, at any rate, she would have furnished them with airtight flaps, such as are the enviable possession of the bat. But, in truth, man is a poor animal like the rest, and his powers are meant only to maintain him in the struggle for existence; so he must need keep his ears always open, to announce of themselves, by night as by day, the approach of the pursuer.

Notes

{1} *Dunciad,* iii, 194. (AS)
{2} *Faust,* I. 329. (AS)
{3} The author refers to whips cracking. See his essay *On Noise.* (TBS)

31
21 Writers to Study for Style

Burnett, Frances Hodgson. *The Secret Garden.*

Butler, Samuel. *The Way of All Flesh;* and *Erewhon;* and *Erewhon Revisited.*

Dickens, Charles. *Great Expectations;* and *Our Mutual Friend.*

Dickinson, Emily. *Poems.*

Fielding, Henry. *Tom Jones.*

Forster, E.M. *A Room With A View.*

Kazantzakis, Nikos. *Zorba The Greek* (The translation by Carl Wildman).

Lawrence, D.H. *Women in Love.*

Nin, Anais. *The Diaries of Anais Nin.*

Sand, George. *Consuelo: A Romance of Venice.* (Zorba Press edition, 2016)

Shaw, George Bernard. *Pygmalion* (the preface, the play, and the sequel).

Shelley, Mary: *Frankenstein — or, The Modern Prometheus.*

Singer, Isaac Bashevis. *The Spinoza of Market Street.*

Swift, Jonathan. *Gulliver's Travels.*

Thoreau, Henry David. *Walde;* and *Life Without Principle.*

Tobias, Michael. *The Adventures of Mr Marigold.* (Zorba Press, 2016)

Twain, Mark (Samuel Clemens). *The Adventures of Huckleberry Finn.*

Ueland, Brenda. *If You Want To Write.*

Wilde, Oscar. *The Picture of Dorian Gray.*

Woolf, Virginia. *A Room of One's Own.*

Yezierska, Anzia. *Hungry Hearts.*

32
Bright Ithaca Reveals
the Mysteries of Literary Style

by Michael Pastore

One warm midnight in July I sauntered to the Commons, where the blue-haired maids of evening chattered purple through my prose. The Commons, in downtown Ithaca, is a three-block-long stretch of walkway and stores, forever closed to traffic, with roofed pavilions for events, tables and chairs for outside dining, and a penny-filled fountain of spraying water in the center of it all. A haven for shoppers, panhandlers, buskers and bohemians, here was every author's dream of the ideal office out-of-doors. I covered the seat of the uncomfortable steel chair with a soft cushion. Onto the top of a round table I dumped two dozen books, one neolithic laptop computer, a biker's water bottle, plastic cups, yellow-highlighting markers, wide-ruled notebooks, and heaps of eraserless pencils and black-inked pens. A white candle, lit by a wooden match, added a spark of elegance to Ithaca's earthy ambience. With a sigh I sat down to answer the tremendous question: How could I write a literary masterpiece, an honest book that would endure?

This Quixotic madness had a method: I promised myself to remain here for twenty-four hours, to study the masters of style. Yet how many light-years now divide the clear old books from the incomprehensible new life! The first book I opened described how Victorian women wore up to thirty-seven pounds of clothing; and the Rational Dress Society was formed to reduce and limit that amount to seven pounds. Around me now — to survive the sweltering heat wave and to attract attractive males — three young ladies, more naked than not, strolled the crowded walkways. The amount of clothing that these women were wearing could be rolled up and stuffed into my drinking cup. For every artist, the first lesson is economy: imitate Nature and discard everything superfluous. Less reveals more. "Vigorous writing is concise" is six too many syllables. Be brief.

A sculptor, when asked, "How do you carve an elephant?", replied truthfully: "I start with a block of marble, and then I cut away everything that does not look like an elephant." Mastery of every art begins when the new artist learns how to cut out the mistakes. Which mistakes? Our three great literary blunders are the obsession with correctness; the confusion between financial success and excellence; and the worship of the cult of the obscure.

Midnight. Hordes of black-clad women and metal-filled men shuffled past my table, breaking the night's silence with ring tones from their celly phones. Like brie-filled mousetraps, ten thousand distractions taunt the creative mind. I read that slim, classic volume about plagiarism: *The Elements of Steal;* then browsed the contents of the obese *Windy City Manual.* Hundreds of pages later sparrows twittered, light opened the sky, and a squad of cleaning tractors rolled up and down the Commons with an ear-breaking din. These books I had assembled were filled with SPUG: Spelling, Punctuation, Usage, Grammar. Ignoring the essentials — precision, power, and passion — the books explained the most trivial facets of the writer's art: how to follow rules and be correct. Bombarding high school and university students with hundreds of generic rules — the same ones taught unsuccessfully for forty years — yielded students who viewed writing as the most boring and unnecessary chore on Earth.

Mastering this SPUG will never bring you one millimeter closer to the flashes of heaven from a Thoreau, the earthy passion of a Kazantzakis, the revolutionary humor of a Shaw, the supercelestial thoughts of a Montaigne. Disappointedly, I bagged the so-called style books, then covered my desk with dollar paperbacks by the ten sublime authors: Homer, Dante, Shakespeare, Cervantes, Goethe, Rabelais, Emerson, Balzac, Dostoyevsky, Tolstoy. Like Robert Louis Stevenson, I would play "the sedulous ape", and study these geniuses in order to glean the secrets of their technique.

Eight morning bells clanged from the campus clock-tower as the bankers hurried through the Commons to their sacred vaults. Wearing pressed pants, white shirts, silver cufflinks, and golden ties, they might have heeded Thoreau — not Henry David, but our contemporary O. Thoreau — who warned: "Avarice is a stunning woman. First she turns your head, then she twists it off at the neck." ... The death of real literature begins when writing is performed for money only. A specter haunts America, the conspiracy to encourage the masses to read the worst of all possible books. Almost everyone participates in this grand deception — authors, editors, booksellers, critics, bloggers, and especially agents and publishers. Fiction on our best-seller lists is unfit for the minds of men or manatees.

What is now called our "literature" — the mirror of who we are and the pole-star of how we might live more peacefully and wisely — is devised by hacks, screened by pimps and published by profiteers. Millions of dollars are wasted promoting novels comprised of recycled plotz, horrific horror, mindless car chases, ludicrous messages embedded in wafers and religious scrolls, middle-aged new agers bumbling through South America seeking demeaning of life, pulp with product placements, anti-scientific propaganda, and bimbos and bodybuilders swept up in the heart-wrenching tornadoes of a trite romance. Occasionally these best-sellers are not so badly written, but always they have nothing to say. Ala the Greek writer who pointed to a parrot, then laughed as he shouted: "You are a voice and nothing more."

The genuine authors of the past were devoted to truth, to raising personal awareness, and to the liberation of humanity from poverty, tyranny, and ignorance. Tolstoy worked five years to create *War and Peace;* and his 20-year-old wife Sonya rewrote the 560,000-word manuscript, by hand, seven times. Goethe labored 30 years to write his drama *Faust.* Rumi's masterpiece *Mathnawi-i-Manawi* (Spiritual Couplets), required 43 years to complete. To get every word just right, Kazantzakis worked full-time on his epic poem *The Odyssey: A Modern Sequel* — for 12 years. Nelson Algren insisted that a writer needs two years to write a good novel. Yet our best-sellers are churned out in mere months, from a mindless formula. Might we dare ask, "Why?" ... Because our spoiled authors are hard-pressed economically to pay for their mansions, cars, and yachts. Writers writing for money write in a hurry. Real authors know that excellence requires time, patience, and poise. They work timelessly, without haste or rest, perfectly aware that *deadlines* are merely one rushed 's' away from *deadliness.* They write spontaneously at first, and then keep polishing until the book glows with the light that is impassioned, personal, unique.

At ten bells, the Commons is invaded by the Academics, laptop bags over their shoulders, left hand holding a tome unreadable, right hand clutching a coffee cup, and mouth gripping a two-dollar pastry filled with sugary creme. Observing this species, something made my mind shift to the subject of obscure writing, writing that cannot be understood by mortal men. Witness the immense pomposity of sesquipedalian verbiage! This bleak communication lies everywhere: from the made-up mouths of politicians seeking to be re-elected and to deceive, to the slick pages of the academic journals whose authors desire the paradise of tenure and the perks of intellectual prestige.

Some of these scribblers blame their failure to communicate on the weakness of language itself. Theorists claim to be helpless inmates condemned to life sentences inside the walls of "the prison house of language." But a genuine writer, a poet or a novelist, reveres "the glorious land of language", and always — by immense work, by pure integrity, by a selflessness that cares nothing for material gain, by a passionate love for humanity and uncompromising devotion to the truth — accomplishes the fertile miracle of communication. "I see one rule," wrote the novelist

Stendhal, "to be clear." And Aristotle agreed, with his famous advice for writers in every genre: "Think like a philosopher, and speak like a common man."

One critic hits the nail on the head, for every thousand critics who hit their heads on the nail. George Orwell, a champion for the cause of lucid writing, explained: "The great enemy of language is insincerity. When there is a gap between one's real and one's declared aims, one turns, as it were, instinctively, to long words and exhausted idioms, like a cuttlefish squirting out ink."

Too much focus on correctness; writing for money only; and writing that is obscure — these are the three great enemies of literary style. These concern the writer's purpose and technique, but never touch the more complex problems revolving around the lives, and the personalities, of the writers themselves. In his beautifully-written book *Enemies of Promise,* Cyril Connolly identifies and discusses the obstacles that prevent writers from writing books that matter. These enemies are: the need for money; the detour into journalistic writing; too much involvement in politics; escapism, into traps such as drinking, daydreaming, and religion; the occupation of marriage and the pre-occupation with sex; and — this above all: the deluding influence of literary success.

At one second before 12 noon some sirens blared, telling the peace-loving Ithacans that it was either Tuesday — when these atavistic alarms were tested — or that a weapon of mass destruction was speeding towards our inconsequential town. I opened some food containers to eat lunch, as aromas from the restaurants added wafts of spiciness to my plain fruit, yogurt, and nuts. The simple life at the Commons requires no high-tech location gadgets: a good nose can tell you precisely where you are. The fragrance of French food flows from the east side; walking westward you smell the marvelous cuisine of Thailand, then the pizzaz of pizza, and then, by the pavilion, the stench of grilled bodies from the vendor of hot dogs and kraut. When your nostrils twitch between the smells of local coffee and imported health-food, you can be certain that you're beside the fountain. Continue to amble toward the west and you detect the scents of french fries, then the sizzle of sushi Japanese, and at last you smell the alcohol reeking from the corner bar. ... For the next hours I was able to ignore these aromatic distractions, to concentrate on reading passages from the ten classic authors and their incomparable books.

By 7 pm I heard sounds of a band tuning their instruments, as the boomer generation strolled to the center pavilion, to listen to music and to dance.

The signs at the Commons indicated an Ithaca filled with intellectual rebels, like Paris during the Enlightenment, or Athens in the age of Pericles. On a bookstore window you see "Shoplifters will be deconstructed." On the walk in front of the religious coffee café, some prankster had scrawled "My messiah can beat up your messiah." More subtle yet, a clothing store sign parodies a line from Emerson, "Thongs are in the saddle and ride mankind." ... A war protester holds a sign that says "Time for Change," beside a homeless man whose sign begs, "Change for Wine" ... The town T-shirts and bumper stickers are also unforgettable: "Ithaca is Gorges" ... "Ithaca is not George's" ... "Defend America: Defeat Bush" ... "If you're not outraged, you're not paying attention." ... And an honest psychological profile of the town, "Ithaca: ten square miles surrounded by reality."

Yet perhaps the good life here has been a bit too good. The counterculture is dried up, rebellion gives way to home-grown veggies sold on Saturdays, and the Green Party members can no longer distinguish between the Democans and the Republicrats. The last cicada shell of earthiness is the vegetarian restaurant too famous to be named. Alas, in this entire ten square miles of unreality, only a few hundred dedicated vegetarians reside.

The moment when the Ithacans started dancing, I changed my tune. A Berkeley of the East our Ithaca is not. Despite its failure as a hub for social change, Ithaca has been good to me. Living a year in Pittsburgh, a month in Piscataway, or thirty minutes in the American South, would send me flying off to Paris as a bohemian expatriate. An artist can live and work in Ithaca, with no need for daydreams of escaping to Europe or Utopia. Ithaca is a haven from the crowded madness of big-city existence. A respite from our culture that spins around money and things. An experiment in *unpopular* culture. And, most remarkably, a model for tolerance and acceptance of all varieties of lifestyles and ideas.

Ithaca has style. On one side of the Commons an African drum is beating; on the other end a slender dark-haired violinist, wearing a pink bandana and a lovely face, fiddles a lively gypsy melody. An 8-year-old girl smiles at me, as she walks past my chair, then sits down on the fountain's ledge and opens a book of essays by Emerson. A waiter at an outdoor restaurant whirls a tray on his fingertips, like a Harlem Globetrotter spinning a basketball. When Nietzsche first met Lou Salome, he whispered to her "From what star hast thou fallen!" ... A city-born artist, arriving in Ithaca after a long journey through Bedlamerica, finds here a balance between crushing poverty and wasteful luxury, a rejuvenating naturalness and calm. Studying this splendid town, with its wondrous waterfalls and gorges, the artist rapturously shouts: "Bright Ithaca! What planet am I on!"

What is style? ... It is more, vastly more, than the sum of the diction (the choice and use of words), the syntax (the arrangement of words in phrases and sentences), and the careful crafting of sentences to transmit an idea or evoke a feeling. Style, in great writing, is the sincerest expression of the author's inmost self. Great style is clear, concise, and captivating — nothing is lacking, nothing is superfluous. Whenever we read great writing something genuine in it moves us, in waves of resonance and recognition, with rays of wonder and delight.

Style is the Zen master's finger pointing at the new moon. Style grabs your attention and holds it fast. Had Nietzsche hastily scribbled the mundane "It is logical to infer that men can never know about the essence and influence of the Divine," — then hardly a bushy eyebrow would have been raised. Instead he takes this same notion, plays with the words, then shouts with defiant enthusiasm, "God is dead and we have killed him!" And in this way the savvy philosopher creates a perennial brouhaha.

Style can never be acquired magically, using simple recipes: dangle your participles, shoot your adjectives, prune your pleonasms, and zap your zeugmas. Style is the man himself, or the woman herself. Writing is good when it is personal; when it captures the vision in the man or woman, and reveals the way she or he sees the world outside. A great poem or novel communicates the essence of the author's radiant inner life. Style matters to some degree. Vision, compassion, your own character, sincerity, living your life intensely and loving life intensely — all matter vastly more than the style.

Water sprays me; little children throw pennies into the fountain and thirsty bagmen fish them out. Sparrows hop on the cement, sip water and peck at crumbs of whole-wheat pizza crust. I notice that a new vegan restaurant has just opened, to honor our dear President, called "Broccoli Obama." Again I opened the beautifully-written book by Cyril Connolly. In the first section, he argues that we need to find a stylistic balance between prose that is too simple and spare, and prose that is too complex and ornate. I heard children laughing, and in one fortuitous flash I realized that even the best books about style lick the peel and toss the banana aside. These books imply that a masterpiece depends on style and not on vision; on language and not on meaning; on the sound of the words and not the truth of the experiences and ideas.

The critics and theorists are blind to the heart of things, but the genuine authors understand. Thoreau, in *Walden,* asks us: "For what are the classics but the noblest recorded thoughts of man?" ... And Tolstoy lucidly explains, "Art is that human activity having for its purpose the transmission of the highest and best feelings to which men have risen."

Ten o'clock and the dancers are done dancing, the barbarians make for the bars. A grey-haired woman waves a poster from a *Village Voice* cover: President Bush is depicted as a vampire, his bloody fangs sucking the neck of the lovely Statue of Liberty. George Bernard Shaw epitomized the type, when (in his play *Caesar and Cleopatra*) he wrote: "Pardon him, Theodotus: he is a barbarian, and thinks that the customs of his tribe and island are the laws of nature."

So how can the modern writer write books that help us to know ourselves, and understand this diverse and complex world? ... He needs to teach himself to write with sincerity, vitality, and clarity. He needs, as Van Wyck Brooks advised, in *The Writer in America,* to avoid the temptation of making language games more significant than meaning. The real writer focuses his energies on "the human element" — he writes books about the most significant joys and struggles of human beings.

For a brief time, in a few moments of being, Virginia Woolf found the answer to the writer's plight. "The way to write well," she said, "is to live intensely." ... Live intensely, and then express this intense life with passion, precision, and sincerity.

The genuine writer is a rebel with a cause. Society needs her to teach us the dangers and the vapidness of our consuming culture, a culture obsessed with money, trite pleasures, material objects, and technologies that dehumanize. The 19th-Century authors John Ruskin and William Morris were centuries ahead of their time. They used the arts to make their world more truthful, more equal economically, more filled with beauty and joy. Art is never for mindless entertainment only; art cannot be the siren's song that makes us ignore or forget our needs and dreams. Art must be revolutionary, and society must be transformed.

Midnight once again at the Ithaca Commons. With new eyes I see this small world fill up with beggars and with punk-clad teenagers, young people with old faces: anxious, distrusting, care-filled, disconnected, lost. Change is good, change is necessary, change is difficult. The force of history and the farce of human folly weighs against us. Some artists encourage us to daydream, others try to wake us from our self-destructive sleep. What happens to these voices in the modern wilderness? Schopenhauer — called by Tolstoy "the greatest genius who ever lived" — wrote: "I would tell of the martyrdom of almost all the great masters of every kind of art ... they lived in poverty and misery, while fame, honor and riches were the lot of the unworthy ... they were kept up by the love of their work."

They were kept up by the love of their work! ... Zora Neale Hurston worked as a maid, died poor and forgotten, and was buried in an unmarked grave. Thoreau sold the pencils that he carved, and made so many that he could reach into a barrel and instantly retrieve exactly one dozen in his hand. Melville — whose *Moby Dick* sold 60 copies in the first ten years — slaved as a clerk to pay debts and support his family. Walt Whitman, at the age of 55, peddled his books of poetry from a handbasket on the Camden streets.

Again I looked at these young persons around me, and I remembered something momentous. For the first time I understood. Are we one family? Would the Earth stop spinning if we lived and loved that way? ... I felt the fierce wrath that I'd forgotten for so many years. I dared myself to begin again, to write with passion and integrity. Tell your truth — all things sacred and all things inhumane — without a shard of fear or compromise. This time I would speak with more sincerity, intensity, audacity. And with relentless efforts and taoist patience — maybe even with a bit more style.

And what will you do — honest Henry, wise Virginia, and sweet Walt — when the cynics scowl and screech: that this world is hopeless beyond hope, that men devour other men like wolves, that the place of a woman is beneath a man, that children must be drugged or beaten into absolute obedience, that Americans improve their minds by watching more TV, that revolutionary books should be banned or burned, that technology alone can solve the planet's problems, that a bushwhacking tyrant should be given all the godlike powers of an emperor, that science should be replaced by religious fairy tales, that good art is powerless to open minds, that the Quixotes of the world are mad, and that to work for equality and justice is to throw water into the sea?

Keep on writing, every morning, and follow the advice of Mrs. Blake: "We will smile sweetly and we will sing."

Michael Pastore
Ithaca, New York, USA

Index

About Zorba Press

Zorba Press is an independent publisher of books, ebooks, audio books, and films on DVDs. From the gorgeous gorges of Ithaca, New York, we publish the paperback books The Zorba Anthology of Love Stories; The Ithaca Manual of Style; the anthology of wise quotations called Zenlightenment; and a wild novel about love and eros (for adults) Thoreau Bound: A Utopian Romance in the Isles of Greece.

Currently, we offer about 50 titles of fiction and non- fiction. Some of our popular books include The Terrestrial Gospel of Nikos Kazantzakis; 50 Benefits of Ebooks: A Thinking Person's Guide to the Digital Reading Revolution; Lark's Magic (a comic novel for children); Sing In Me, Muse, and Through Me Tell the Story: Greek Culture Performed by Maria Hnaraki; and the first paperback and ebook editions of a colossal modern classic, all 625,000 words of Michael Tobias's extraordinary novel, The Adventures of Mr Marigold.

Our most recent publications are Kazantzakis: A Film By Michael Tobias (video on DVD); the paperback My Life On The Ragged Paths Of Pan: Selected Poems and Translations of Thanasis Maskaleris; and Sappho At The Edge Of Love: 100 Poems by Michael Pastore (paperback and ebook and audiobook).

At Zorba Press, we practice what we call "Sustainable Publishing": publishing with a deeper sense of awareness, compassion, and responsibility. Zorba's mission is to promote the innovative ideas and the daring books that nourish children and childhood, point the way to a culture of non-violence, create a sustainable future, and nurture — for every living being — a new world of love, kindness, courage, creativity, sincerity, and peace.

Visit Zorba Press at

www.ZorbaPress.com

www.ingramcontent.com/pod-product-compliance
Lightning Source LLC
Chambersburg PA
CBHW020156090426
42734CB00008B/835